I AM . . .

Identity Crisis Undone
—the Discovery of
Who We
Are Through
the Eyes of God.

ADRIENE LAW

WESTBOW
PRESS®
A DIVISION OF THOMAS NELSON
& ZONDERVAN

Scripture quotations marked (NIV) are taken from the Holy Bible, New International Version®,
NIV®. Copyright © 1973, 1978, 1984, 2011 by Biblica, Inc.™ Used by permission of Zondervan.
All rights reserved worldwide. www.zondervan.com The "NIV" and "New International Version"
are trademarks registered in the United States Patent and Trademark Office by Biblica, Inc.™

Scripture quotations marked (NKJV) are taken from the New King James Version®.
Copyright © 1982 by Thomas Nelson. Used by permission. All rights reserved.

Scripture quotations marked (NLT) are taken from the Holy Bible, New Living Translation,
copyright ©1996, 2004, 2007, 2013, 2015 by Tyndale House Foundation. Used by permission
of Tyndale House Publishers, Inc., Carol Stream, Illinois 60188. All rights reserved.

Scripture quotations marked MSG are taken from THE MESSAGE, copyright © 1993,
1994, 1995, 1996, 2000, 2001, 2002 by Eugene H. Peterson. Used by permission of
NavPress. All rights reserved. Represented by Tyndale House Publishers, Inc.

Scripture quotations taken from the Amplified® Bible (AMP),
Copyright © 2015 by The Lockman Foundation
Used by permission. www.Lockman.org.

WestBow Press books may be ordered through booksellers or by contacting:

WestBow Press
A Division of Thomas Nelson & Zondervan
1663 Liberty Drive
Bloomington, IN 47403
www.westbowpress.com
1 (866) 928-1240

Because of the dynamic nature of the Internet, any web addresses or links contained
in this book may have changed since publication and may no longer be valid. The views
expressed in this work are solely those of the author and do not necessarily reflect the
views of the publisher, and the publisher hereby disclaims any responsibility for them.

Any people depicted in stock imagery provided by Thinkstock are models,
and such images are being used for illustrative purposes only.
Certain stock imagery © Thinkstock.

ISBN: 978-1-5127-8032-1 (sc)
ISBN: 978-1-5127-8033-8 (hc)
ISBN: 978-1-5127-8031-4 (e)

Library of Congress Control Number: 2017904405

Print information available on the last page.

WestBow Press rev. date: 05/16/2017

This book is dedicated to each
and every life it touches.

You're beautiful from head to toe, my dear love,
beautiful beyond compare, absolutely flawless.
—Song of Solomon 4:7 (MSG)

With special thanks to
my loving and supportive husband, Steven:
You are and have been an incredible encourager on this journey;
I love growing with you, together and through each other, in Christ,
and I pray we always will.

Above all, have fervent and unfailing love for one another,
because love covers a multitude of sins;
it overlooks unkindness and unselfishly seeks the best for others.
—1 Peter 4:8 (AMP)

To my daughters, Heather and Hayley:
Never forget how much you are loved.
You are both amazing and precious gifts
that God has blessed me with.
Always grow in your strengths and passions and in Christ.
And trust that God will always lead you,
even when life doesn't make sense.

Trust in the Lord with all your heart;
do not depend on your own understanding.
Seek his will in all you do,
and he will show you which path to take.
—Proverbs 3:5–6 (NLT)

CONTENTS

INTRODUCTION

The two most impacting words we will ever say are "I am" because whatever follows them is what we believe.

Since 2010, I have been on a journey of discovery, of finding out who I am, particularly who I am in the eyes of God.

I listened to notable, godly, generous pastors and preachers from all over the world; they said, "When you know who you are in Christ, *then* …," but no one ever really went into all that. They would teach and preach about what happens "then" but never about who I was, or who *we* are as children of God—just that once I knew who I was, a whole new level of God would open up: the "then."

At that time, and in that place, I didn't know who I was—literally or spiritually—and I yearned to know. In fact, I needed to know. How I thought of myself at that time was really was not a good place to be. So my journey began.

Underneath my skin and buried somewhere deep in my soul, I knew I was a good and decent person, but for the life of me, I could not figure out why I was here or why I had to endure so much in my life. I had no purpose, felt no value, and saw little worth in myself.

With each failure, I felt defeated, and as the failures mounted up, they took me to deeper and deeper levels of despair. I would end up in great darkness, yet always sensing in my spirit that there had to be more than this in the world. Waves would crash around me, sometimes throwing me against the rocks. Life's curve balls would hit me and almost take me out. By the time I was a teenager, I already wore the labels that said "Hello, my name is Failure, Mistake, Unwanted, Worthless, Unloved, and Rejected." And I wore them for most of my life.

In spite of my best efforts and within my own strength, energy, and power, I tried to shake these labels and prove to someone, to anyone, that I was not these things; that I had value, worth, and purpose. But then the waves would crash me into the rocks again.

There isn't much that hasn't happened to me, whether by my poor choices or by others, things that no one should have to go through or endure, particularly as a woman. And when I would read Romans 8:28, which says that God works all things together for the good of those who love Him and are called according to His purpose, I would wonder how on earth He could tie all my messes and mistakes into anything good.

I think we often see God as this mean, controlling, vengeful being who just allows all this bad stuff to happen (in the world and to us personally) and does nothing about it. Especially for those who grew up with any amount of religion, we tend to see the God of the Old Testament, who sends floods to wipe people out or locusts to destroy crops and has already banished us all to hell. For a lot of years, hell is pretty much where I lived (or at least decided to visit for a very long time).

When I started to see things through the lens of the cross, the cross of Jesus, I saw a completely different God. I saw a Father Who loves *all* His creation—including myself. And when I stopped blaming Him for everything I had ever endured or done, and started embracing His vision of me, it was (and still is) a very powerful perspective.

Looking at life and myself through the lens of the cross, discovering how God saw me, even in all my mess, I started speaking His word over myself, and my life started changing—and changing in extremely positive ways.

Now, when I look back on it all, I see God's hand all over my life, even when I was so far away from Him, but also when I hadn't even come to Him yet.

I am not a pastor, nor am I exceedingly educated, and I don't have all the answers. I am wife, a mom, a daughter, a sister, a friend, and most certainly an ever-growing, ever-evolving Christ-follower. Yet I know this: We have a very real enemy out there, someone who does not want us to reach our potential, our purpose, or indeed who we were created to be. Our enemy is the one who wants us to stay where we are in despair, misery, failure, or addiction, filled with blame and hate (or whatever it is that we fear). Yet we were never designed to be living that way.

Living under God's protective, enduring, unfailing, peaceful, and freeing love *is* how we were designed to be. We were created to live fruitful, thriving lives filled with love, joy, peace, hope, goodness, faithfulness, patience, and kindness for one another. We were designed to be connected, to belong, and to be loved.

I have compiled this book to encourage you, help you, and reach that spirit within you that only God can reach. I'm not rewriting the Bible; I'm tying my experiences and my life into scriptures which stand out to me with and for each statement. The words I'm using are my own words, yet each one is exactly as God sees each of us. We are each unique, but we are also the same in His eyes; no one is greater or lesser.

God's word is powerful. Discovering who you really are in and through Christ, and who you really are to God, is a powerful journey: a journey of forgiveness, redemption, freedom, and joy; a journey that leads to heaven and escapes the hells we can experience in our everyday lives; a journey that leads to a brand new perspective of you. So my hope, my prayer, my dream, and my purpose with this book is to reach people who have experienced trials, defeats, and losses; who feel less than they really are; who are perhaps lost and don't know the way out ... because that's where I was.

I am convinced with an all-consuming conviction in my heart that when we as a world see who we are meant to be and who we were created to be, then mental health and addiction issues will evaporate, depression and despair will disappear from society, people will stop hating and blaming one another, and our world will indeed find peace. But it starts with each of us, and it starts inside of us. It is a journey from the inside out, and it is a journey of progress; human perfection is an illusion. May God be with you each and every step of the way, and may you find your glory and God's glory at the end of it.

You are worth every single word written in this book; indeed, you are meant to wear *these* labels, the labels God calls you, whether you feel like it or even believe Him right now.

PART 1

PART I

I Am … Amazing

I am marvelous. I am wonderfully made. I am a work of art. Those are incredibly bold things to think of myself, and honestly, there are days when I can look at myself through my own eyes, and I really don't see it.

I used to think that I had way too much garbage in my past and indeed inside of me to ever be considered anything but that garbage. Too many words had been spoken to me and over me which said I was nothing but a failure, worthless, useless, good for nothing, would never amount to anything … not forgetting a whole bunch of expletives that cannot be published in this book.

For too much of my life, whether life was going well or not so well, I lived under those banners. They were ingrained into my being.

Now, today, what I am learning to accept, what this whole "I am …" journey is about, is that those were *not* Your words, Lord. Your words describe me as this marvelous, wonderfully made, amazing work of art. You are describing what You see in me. The me You created, not the me I became.

Throughout this journey called life, the more I see things through the lens of the cross, the more clarity I have, and the more amazing I actually become. You don't make mistakes, and as You made me, that means I am not a mistake. I am indeed Your work of art, and You are my master craftsman, perfectly transforming me into this amazing person, not in a conceited or an arrogant way, just into the person You always intended and designed me to be, to live the life You always planned for me to live.

It feels really good to be Your special possession, knowing there is absolutely nothing good You withhold from me and that I fit together perfectly for what You prepared for me to do. You are indeed an amazing, generous God. And having been made in Your image, that means I am indeed amazing too. I never saw that before.

So today, I am embracing this amazing life that You have given me. I'm embracing this amazing person You designed me to be. I am embracing the amazing future You have set in place for me to have. I am Your marvelous work, and my soul knows that very well. Thank You, Lord, for giving me this amazing view of myself. Thank You for never giving up on me and lifting me up to be the amazing me that You see. Bless You, Lord.

~ ~ ~ ~

I will praise You, for I am fearfully and wonderfully made; marvelous are Your works, and that my soul knows very well.

—Psalm 139:14 (NKJV)

For we are His workmanship His own master work, a work of art, created in Christ Jesus reborn from above—spiritually transformed, renewed, ready to be used for good works, which God prepared for us beforehand taking paths which He set, so that we would walk in them living the good life which He prearranged and made ready for us.

—Ephesians 2:10 (AMP)

He makes the whole body fit together perfectly. As each part does its own special work, it helps the other parts grow, so that the whole body is healthy and growing and full of love.

—Ephesians 4:16 (NLT)

But you are a chosen people, a royal priesthood, a holy nation, God's special possession, that you may declare the praises of him who called you out of darkness into his wonderful light.

—1 Peter 2:9 (NIV)

I Am ... Brand New

Like a piece of clay being modeled into something new, You are making me new, brand new. Externally, I look the same. But internally, I can see it and I can feel it.

Something has changed. It's a different feeling than before; it feels like a freedom almost, like something has been broken off. What has gone and is indeed still disappearing are all the things You never wanted to be there. You are removing all the guilt, all the shame, all the condemnation, and all the rejections. You are taking away the abandonment, the abuse, the senses failures left inside. You are even eliminating fear.

You're doing something here, Lord; I can feel it. I feel new blood coursing through my veins and a new conscience inside of me: a compass, a voice. Something I have never felt before. There is a new boldness about me, a freedom and a peace, a peace that just changes everything I have ever known or understood.

I feel like a little baby again, so excited about having just taken my first step. And You're there. You're cheering me on, saying, "Come to me; you can do it." And I want to; I really want to. I never want to let go of the newness I feel. This freedom is amazing.

I have tears of joy, and my heart is leaping. Is this what it means to be with You? To have all the yucky stuff of my life just washed away? I am refreshed and clean, like I've just had my first shower in two weeks. I never want to leave You and I always want to stay this way, feeling clean and feeling joy.

There's a new connection inside; it's a hotline straight to You. You ... You are coursing through my veins and through my heart. You are washing it all away. Your Spirit is creating in me a new life and a new joy.

I thought before that I needed to be perfect, that You would frown on me, but You aren't. It's welcoming, and it feels like the perfect home. No yelling, no fighting, no feeling condemnation or shame.

It's peaceful; it's joyous. You are so gracious, like I never ever knew before. Even if someone had told me in the past, this is an experience I have never had before. Your Spirit inside is creating something new. Thank You, Jesus. I feel completely changed and brand new.

~ ~ ~ ~

Do not remember the former things, or ponder the things of the past. Listen carefully, I am about to do a new thing, now it will spring forth; will you not be aware of it? I will even put a road in the wilderness, rivers in the desert.

—Isaiah 43:18–19 (AMP)

Jesus said, "You're not listening. Let me say it again. Unless a person submits to this original creation—the 'wind-hovering-over-the-water' creation, the invisible moving the visible, a baptism into a new life—it's not possible to enter God's kingdom. When you look at a baby, it's just that: a body you can look at and touch. But the person who takes shape within is formed by something you can't see and touch—the Spirit—and becomes a living spirit. "So don't be so surprised when I tell you that you have to be 'born from above'—out of this world, so to speak. You know well enough how the wind blows this way and that. You hear it rustling through the trees, but you have no idea where it comes from or where it's headed next. That's the way it is with everyone 'born from above' by the wind of God, the Spirit of God."

—John 3:5–8 (MSG)

Therefore, if anyone is in Christ, he is a new creation; old things have passed away; behold, all things have become new. Now all things are of God, who has reconciled us to Himself through Jesus Christ, and has given us the ministry of reconciliation, that is, that God was in Christ reconciling the world to Himself, not imputing their trespasses to them, and has committed to us the word of reconciliation.

—2 Corinthians 5:17–19 (NKJV)

I Am ... A Child of God

Being a child of someone should indicate that I belong to that person. It should bring up memories of love, inclusion, rejoicing, encouragement, teaching, patience; the list goes on. But for me, and for probably many, it doesn't. In fact, it probably involves the antonyms of all those words: the opposite.

So when I think of being a child, I can often go to those things, but I have learned and indeed am still learning that being a child of God is nothing like anything I have experienced on earth, primarily because You are not earthly. You're in heaven, You're in the wind, You're in all that You created, but You are not earthly.

You are far above and beyond my wildest imaginations, hopes, and dreams, and that means being Your child is too. It's an outrageously unreal concept for many to grasp, and that's part of what makes You who You are and, through You, who I am.

It has never been about what we have, all this stuff that we strive for that makes us who we are. It's always been about what's inside of us and what has been deposited in to us.

I was fortunate enough to have a great father. My dad truly loved me, yet he was a workaholic. He was rarely around. He strived for his family, and we still reap the benefits of his hard work today. But for many, Lord, they didn't have a dad, or what they experienced of their dad wasn't good.

It is easier for me to think of You as my Father and myself as Your child than others, because my earthly experiences with him were good. And still, when I lean in to You, when I discover what being Your child really means, when I am depositing You into me and becoming the me You created me to be. I am Your child. Yours alone.

No matter where I have come from or what I have done. In Your word, Lord, You say that you will be a father, and we will be sons and daughters to You.

Regardless of what my experience has been from an earthly or worldly perspective, Yours is greater, higher, and somehow easier. I don't strive for Your attention. You are always right here with me. You always comfort and encourage me; You always see the best in me. You just simply and easily connect with me and call me Your child.

~ ~ ~ ~

But to all who believed him and accepted him, he gave the right to become children of God.

—John 1:12 (NLT)

For all who are led by the Spirit of God are children of God. So you have not received a spirit that makes you fearful slaves. Instead, you received God's Spirit when he adopted you as his own children. Now we call him, "Abba, Father." For his Spirit joins with our spirit to affirm that we are God's children.

—Romans 8:14–16 (NLT)

For you who are born-again have been reborn from above—spiritually transformed, renewed, sanctified and are all children of God set apart for His purpose with full rights and privileges through faith in Christ Jesus.

—Galatians 3:26 (AMP)

For you were once darkness, but now you are light in the Lord. Walk as children of light (for the fruit of the Spirit is in all goodness, righteousness, and truth), finding out what is acceptable to the Lord.

—Ephesians 5:8–10 (NKJV)

Behold what manner of love the Father has bestowed on us, that we should be called children of God! Therefore the world does not know us, because it did not know Him.

—1 John 3:1 (NKJV)

I Am ... Forgiven

Wow! Forgiven? Really? Even with all I have done? That's amazing, Lord. And what I find so incredible is that You just do it. You do it freely because You love me, and You know that I cannot move forward in any way with this massive weight of guilt and shame around me.

Even growing up and not always doing things wrong, I was wrong. It was just something I was. A mistake. And You even forgive me for thinking and believing that.

It's not that You forgive me of this or that, the small, insignificant things; You have no scale of what things are bigger or smaller than others. In Your eyes, wrong is wrong, period. And it does not matter what I have done. You forgive it all. It's all gone; it's washed away, now and forever. Lord, that is pretty amazing.

When the past creeps back up on me, and there's that voice inside screaming about all I have done and wanting to drag me back there with guilt and shame, You offer me a place called forgiven. I just need to rest and acknowledge that You have indeed forgiven me for it all.

The moment I came to You, You forgave me. It didn't hinge on anything. You didn't ask me to do anything except come to You and leave all that behind. So in those moments, I need to leave that guilt and shame, all my wrongness and wrong thinking, at the foot of the cross and embrace You even more.

My true remorse for the things I have done leads to this incredible change. I no longer want to live in such a manner anymore. I want to connect with You more and more because the grace you continually and constantly shower on to me is just so incredible.

You never sought justice with me for all I've done. You wanted my heart and pledged a relationship with me. You wanted to show me that I was forgiven. You wanted to show me that I could be and should be forgiven and made new.

You took all my stuff with you to the cross and literally nailed it there for me to be this way: forgiven.

~ ~ ~ ~

And He said to them, "This is My blood of the new covenant, My blood which is being poured out for many for the forgiveness of sins."
—Mark 14:24 (AMP)

Therefore, my friends, I want you to know that through Jesus the forgiveness of sins is proclaimed to you.
—Acts 13:38 (NIV)

For he has rescued us from the kingdom of darkness and transferred us into the Kingdom of his dear Son, who purchased our freedom and forgave our sins.
—Colossians 1:13–14 (NLT)

You were dead because of your sins and because your sinful nature was not yet cut away. Then God made you alive with Christ, for he forgave all our sins.
—Colossians 2:13 (NLT)

I am writing to you, dear children, because your sins have been forgiven on account of his name.
—1 John 2:12 (NIV)

I Am ... Loved

When you live a life of basically not feeling loved, it can be really hard to understand and to grasp that anyone would lay down their life for you in love. We come from parents who didn't care, we have experienced self-absorbed people who abused us, and we have been neglected and rejected.

I always thought You were this God of perfection whose expectations I would never ever meet because I just failed at everything.

Even today, it's hard to sometimes comprehend just how much You love us all and how You would have endured the cross for even just one of us. I know that I could not survive one day now without the love of the God of love, and nor would I want to. Nothing can separate me from You, no matter what I do and no matter what life throws at me now.

Satan can come at me with all guns blazing, and I get to hide behind You. You take his bullets for me. People can hate me, bully me, and ridicule me, and You are there with arms wide open, comforting me with a huge hug, telling me that I'm okay and it will all be okay.

You are absolute, perfect love. You don't judge me. You don't shame me. You don't condemn me. You don't bully me. You don't even want anything from me.

You just love me and always have. You actually believe that I can be something in this world. You encourage me every day. You wash away my yesterdays and give me hope for tomorrow.

You saw my worth, value, gifts, and capabilities when no one else did. You saw someone You wanted to literally give Your life to, and You taught me what love really looks like. It's self-less, not selfish. It's giving, loyal, forgiving, patient, trusting, hopeful, faithful, respectful, and freeing.

I tried so hard for so long to find love, and then Your love found me. And I have never, ever felt so free or loved, Lord. Thank You for blessing me with Your sacrifice, Jesus. You have set me free and shown me a true, unrelenting, selfless, loyal, gracious love.

~ ~ ~ ~

For God so loved the world that He gave His only begotten Son, that whoever believes in Him should not perish but have everlasting life. For God did not send His Son into the world to condemn the world, but that the world through Him might be saved. He who believes in Him is not condemned; but he who does not believe is condemned already, because he has not believed in the name of the only begotten Son of God.

—John 3:16–18 (NKJV)

And I am convinced that nothing can ever separate us from God's love. Neither death nor life, neither angels nor demons, neither our fears for today nor our worries about tomorrow—not even the powers of hell can separate us from God's love. No power in the sky above or in the earth below—indeed, nothing in all creation will ever be able to separate us from the love of God that is revealed in Christ Jesus our Lord.

—Romans 8:38–39 (NLT)

But God, being so very rich in mercy, because of His great and wonderful love with which He loved us, even when we were spiritually dead and separated from Him because of our sins, He made us spiritually alive together with Christ (for by His grace—His undeserved favor and mercy—you have been saved from God's judgment).

—Ephesians 2:4–5 (AMP)

My old self has been crucified with Christ. It is no longer I who live, but Christ lives in me. So I live in this earthly body by trusting in the Son of God, who loved me and gave himself for me.

—Galatians 2:20 (NLT)

I Am ... Saved

Lord, You are way more than any religion has to offer. I am saved through a relationship with You. You, the God of this world, creator of all the heavens and of earth, actually humbled Yourself from the heights of heaven, entered into this world as a baby, grew as a man, showed us the way You intended us to live, and then went to the cross to save us from even ourselves.

You came as a servant, not as a Lord. You came to reach the sick, the poor, the needy, the oppressed; not those who knew it all and thought they were better than others.

Until I realized all this, until I actually started to see everything through the lens of Your cross, until I started to see just how incredibly loved I was by You, nothing in my life made any sense whatsoever.

You didn't come to condemn me. You came to save me. In You, through You, and by You, I am saved.

When I enter Your gates, I find massive freedom, peace, and deliverance. All my bondage is taken away. Everything that ever kept me captive, including my own mind, is transformed into something radiant.

My life has purpose and meaning. I have joy. There is peace in my world even when there isn't peace in this world. You never put me to shame, and You always want nothing but the very best for me. Being saved by You, having You reach down to my level, is an experience like no other.

You ask nothing from me, just a relationship with You. You desire to walk with me, where I am, yet not wanting me to stay in my ditch. You lift me out, dust me off, and say, "Hey, I'm here, let's try this thing again."

It's never been about what I can or can't do; it has always been (and will always be) about what You did, can do, and want to do. You came to set the captives free, and in so many ways, ways we cannot even comprehend, we are captives of this world and of an enemy who wants to keep us where we are: in the prisons we created.

Yet those who see the real You find in themselves the real me: the free me, the perfect me, the saved me. It's not hard, for You made it easy. And You wanted to save me. Your grace found me, and Your grace saved me. The greatest gift of them all: being saved.

~ ~ ~ ~

I am the door. If anyone enters by Me, he will be saved, and will go in and out and find pasture.

—John 10:9 (NKJV)

Much more then, having now been justified by His blood, we shall be saved from wrath through Him. For if when we were enemies we were reconciled to God through the death of His Son, much more, having been reconciled, we shall be saved by His life.

—Romans 5:9–10 (NKJV)

If you declare with your mouth, "Jesus is Lord," and believe in your heart that God raised him from the dead, you will be saved. For it is with your heart that you believe and are justified, and it is with your mouth that you profess your faith and are saved. As Scripture says, "Anyone who believes in him will never be put to shame."

—Romans 10:9–11 (NIV)

For by grace you have been saved through faith, and that not of yourselves; it is the gift of God, not of works, lest anyone should boast.

—Ephesians 2:8–9 (NKJV)

I Am ... Valued

I have been so reckless in some choices I've made. I have not had great value for my life because I never felt valued in this world. Failure, Mistake, Unwanted, Unloved were labels I carried with me for so long. I did not value myself like You value me. Lord, I didn't even like myself.

As I grew up, I realized that I didn't measure up, and my value and self-worth decreased with each comment, each rejection, each mental injury, and each emotional deflation. Encouragement was something so foreign to me. And for sure I learned how little value I seemed to have.

So coming from that to where I am now, along this journey with You, value is something that You are placing into me daily.

Each day, You actually bless me with something, some incident or revelation of just how valuable I am to You. My value is now completely rooted in You. You know every single inch of me; every cell was created by You.

How did I not see that before, that You actually care about me and want me to rejoice in this life and triumph? You have crowns lined up for me and want me to be honored and be honorable. You chose me, You created me, You want me, and You value me.

You don't want me living with shame, guilt, hurt, or regret. You want me living with peace, freedom, and everlasting joy. You lead me in right ways, honorable ways, glorious ways. You bless me and prosper me in ways that I could have never, ever imagined.

When I look back on my life, I can now see that You had Your hand guiding me and protecting me, even though I stupidly wandered into dangerous places or indeed before I had ever even come to You. You were there.

You saw a child You valued, and You relentlessly pursued me with Your loving hand, wanting me to be crowned with righteousness: Your righteousness. You have spent my entire life showing me how much You valued me, and I see that now. I am valued by the most glorious and loving God, when for most of my life, I felt little value even for myself.

Thank You, Lord, for lifting me up, raising me higher, helping me find joy, and labeling me valued.

~ ~ ~ ~

Instead of your shame you shall have double honor, and instead of confusion they shall rejoice in their portion. Therefore in their land they shall possess double; everlasting joy shall be theirs.

—Isaiah 61:7 (NKJV)

Now thanks be to God who always leads us in triumph in Christ, and through us diffuses the fragrance of His knowledge in every place. For we are to God the fragrance of Christ among those who are being saved and among those who are perishing.

—2 Corinthians 2:14–15 (NKJV)

Now there is in store for me the crown of righteousness, which the Lord, the righteous Judge, will award to me on that day—and not only to me, but also to all who have longed for his appearing.

—2 Timothy 4:8 (NIV)

Blessed happy, spiritually prosperous, favored by God is the man who is steadfast under trial and perseveres when tempted; for when he has passed the test and been approved, he will receive the victor's crown of life which the Lord has promised to those who love Him.

—James 1:12 (AMP)

But you are a chosen people, a royal priesthood, a holy nation, God's special possession, that you may declare the praises of him who called you out of darkness into his wonderful light.

—1 Peter 2:9 (NIV)

Heavenly Father, I come to You in prayer asking for the forgiveness of my sins. I confess with my mouth and believe in my heart that Jesus is Your Son and that He died on a cross for me, so that I could be forgiven, have new life, and have eternal life with You.

Jesus, I believe that You rose from the dead, and I ask You right now to come into my life, live in my heart, and be my personal Lord and Savior. I am tired of doing it my way. Help me start doing things Your way. Fill the emptiness in me with Your Holy Spirit, and make me whole. Jesus, I believe! Help me to trust You, Lord. Help me to love You and live for You. Help me to understand your mercy, grace, and peace. Thank You, Lord. In Jesus' name, I pray. Amen.

PART 2

I AM ... ABLE

Sometimes, Lord, I just need to relax and know that it is You in me Who is in control. I need to get out of Your way and allow You to grow me and work in me so that in You, I can indeed do all the amazing things You have predestined me to do.

I have spent far too long trying to spin my wheels to get this or that done, to get into a situation or indeed out of one. My life has been crazy. It's been chasing after this or trying to escape from that.

But honestly, the only place I am truly able to do anything is in and with You. When I give it all to You, You actually empower me to do whatever it is You have put before me. If it's letting go of something, You make me able, through Your strength. If it's something I'm supposed to walk through, You are there with me. My confidence comes from Your ability, not mine.

So I am sinking myself into Your word and have faith in You. The answer is always found in You: Your word, Your promises, Your faithfulness, and my trust and faith in all of those. You never, ever give me more than I can handle.

You give me grace each day, and each day, it is just enough to get me through that day. Never too little and never too much; just perfect grace, in the perfect amount. You lead me to rest. You lead me in the right ways.

Yes, sometimes I need to wait. I need to have patience, and I need to grow. I am learning how to walk in Your ways and trust You through each moment, each hour, and each day. I am believing that You are able and that through You, I am able.

I thank You, Lord, for giving me that strength, growing that strength in me, and showing me that through You, I can run this race. I am able, one step at a time, to run this race by just putting one foot in front of the other and looking to You.

In my dark places, You are the light and the hope in front of me. In my triumphs, as I overcome temptations, You are the one I thank for giving me the ability to do it. You are gracious and faithful, and You make me able. I am able to rest and to trust, and I am reassured that You are with me, triumph after triumph (and indeed, hiccup after hiccup).

You celebrate with me in victories, and You strengthen my spirit and my faith when I stumble, growing me constantly in my abilities and trust. Thank You for always being faithful.

~ ~ ~ ~

When He went into the house, the blind men came up to Him, and Jesus said to them, "Do you believe with a deep, abiding trust that I am able to do this?" They said to Him, "Yes, Lord."

—Matthew 9:28 (AMP)

Abraham never wavered in believing God's promise. In fact, his faith grew stronger, and in this he brought glory to God. He was fully convinced that God is able to do whatever he promises.

—Romans 4:20–21 (NLT)

No test or temptation that comes your way is beyond the course of what others have had to face. All you need to remember is that God will never let you down; he'll never let you be pushed past your limit; he'll always be there to help you come through it. So, my very dear friends, when you see people reducing God to something they can use or control, get out of their company as fast as you can.

—1 Corinthians 10:13–14 (MSG)

Not that I speak in regard to need, for I have learned in whatever state I am, to be content: I know how to be abased, and I know how to abound. Everywhere and in all things I have learned both to be full and to be hungry, both to abound and to suffer need. I can do all things through Christ who strengthens me.

—Philippians 4:11–13 (NKJV)

I Am … Blameless

Oh, this is a biggie, Lord. This is a very bold statement for me to be making, considering everything I have ever done in my life. I was not good, nor was I godly. I was so very far away from You. I still make mistakes every single day and am far from perfect. But that is my worldly view of myself.

Your view of me is so very different. You don't see my dirt, my baggage, my hurts, my hang-ups. You see this magnificent creation that You created: free from sin, free from the world and its clutches. You see light and love. You see holy and blameless.

It's not that I'm right; it's that You are right, and Your perspective over everything is greater than all others because at the end of it all, You are the One we are accountable to. When I am with You, when I put You first, You keep me on the right path so that we will all be blameless before You.

Nothing I do as Your child and in Your will is done in vain, and even as I am growing and learning more and more of what all that actually means, You strengthen me and my heart so that I can continue on the path before me: my journey, my very personal journey with You. And You do that for each of Your children on their very personal journey with You.

There are days when I struggle with that voice in my head, reminding me of all the mistakes I've made and all the people I've hurt and telling me that I will never amount to anything; ridiculing me and condemning me. But that's not You.

You are gentle, peaceful, and quiet. You lead by nudging me along, not screaming in my head. You help me shine. You are polishing me every day so that my light, the light of You, can actually shine in the darkness.

You chose me before the world. You chose all us before the world, to be without fault. Fault comes from our enemy. So I do hold fast to Your word, the life-giving truth of who I am, who we all are, to complete this journey with integrity, peace, even honor: blameless in Your sight.

~ ~ ~ ~

He will also keep you firm to the end, so that you will be blameless on the day of our Lord Jesus Christ. God is faithful, who has called you into fellowship with his Son, Jesus Christ our Lord.

—1 Corinthians 1:8–9 (NIV)

Even before he made the world, God loved us and chose us in Christ to be holy and without fault in his eyes.

—Ephesians 1:4 (NLT)

Do all things without complaining and disputing, that you may become blameless and harmless, children of God without fault in the midst of a crooked and perverse generation, among whom you shine as lights in the world, holding fast the word of life, so that I may rejoice in the day of Christ that I have not run in vain or labored in vain.

—Philippians 2:14–16 (NKJV)

May he strengthen your hearts so that you will be blameless and holy in the presence of our God and Father when our Lord Jesus comes with all his holy ones.

—1 Thessalonians 3:13 (NIV)

Now may the God of peace Himself sanctify you completely; and may your whole spirit, soul, and body be preserved blameless at the coming of our Lord Jesus Christ.

—1 Thessalonians 5:23 (NKJV)

I Am ... Connected

I think we often believe that when we come to Christ, we assume that our whole world is going to instantaneously change. We accept Christ's invitation into a relationship with Him one day and expect to wake up the next day to zero problems, issues, or trials.

It can be very confusing (and sometimes disheartening) when we find our families are still the same, our work is still the same, our circumstances are still the same. I know I sure felt that way.

I could not understand why it was all the same. What was going on? I thought God loved me. Why is all this still happening? For me, it was actually heartbreaking and took me to a place of questioning everything.

But in the end, that was really good for me. I began to see and realize over time that it was me who had the encounter with You and not everyone around me.

In fact, many people around me did not embrace the encounter I had with You. I faced even more hatred, ridicule, and rejection instead of the encouragement I had longed for. I saw, for maybe the first time, a revelation of where people around me really were within themselves and towards me. I saw the loathing from people who were supposed to love me; they did not want me to change, to be free, or to be better (or indeed healthy mentally, physically, or spiritually).

But from the very moment I accepted Christ into my heart and life, I knew that something was new inside of me, that I was connected to this new person, place, or spirit. And the newness I felt inside gave me an internal revival, a hope and sense of belonging to something. In spite of my circumstances being the same, I was different; I was connected.

As I got to know You and entered into a real relationship with You, I knew that in spite of everything that happens around me, You happen inside of me. Your Spirit connected with mine, lifting me up, reviving my heart, giving me true life: a life I really want to live.

And through all that, through my connection with You, my life does indeed change around me. My connection with You shows me who I am and who they are. And Lord, I am so grateful for that. I'm grateful that I have a go-to Person, and that the Holy Spirit is right here with me at all times. My connection with You is indeed a lifeline that I cannot live without. Thank You, Lord.

~ ~ ~ ~

He shall be like a tree planted by the rivers of water, that brings forth its fruit in its season, whose leaf also shall not wither; and whatever he does shall prosper.

—Psalm 1:3 (NKJV)

Those who are planted in the house of the Lord shall flourish in the courts of our God.

—Psalm 92:13 (NKJV)

Abide in Me, and I in you. As the branch cannot bear fruit of itself, unless it abides in the vine, neither can you, unless you abide in Me. I am the vine, you are the branches. He who abides in Me, and I in him, bears much fruit; for without Me you can do nothing.

—John 15:4–5 (NKJV)

Then Christ will make his home in your hearts as you trust in him. Your roots will grow down into God's love and keep you strong.

—Ephesians 3:17 (NLT)

Let your roots grow down into him, and let your lives be built on him. Then your faith will grow strong in the truth you were taught, and you will overflow with thankfulness.

—Colossians 2:7 (NLT)

I Am ... Essential

Growing up feeling less than worthy or valued made it hard to believe that anyone would think of me as essential. We come from so many different backgrounds, and life has taken us all into very different places. Even those with what seem like perfect upbringings can encounter things in life that sideswipe them into some place they never thought they would be.

With me, I don't think I handled any of them very well. They just seemed to knock me down, time after time.

Experiencing the death of someone I truly loved and admired, for instance, took me out of action for a long time. Depression sunk in deep, and even though I was a mother to the two babies You blessed with, I would never have called myself "essential." I was able to function enough to clothe and feed them, the bare necessities, but I was far from what I would have described as a real mom to them during that time.

But it was during this time that I started to really encounter You, Lord. I had already accepted Your Son as my Savior, yet I wasn't really in any type of relationship with You. And interestingly enough, when You started to really show Yourself to me, when You revealed true miracles in my life, I got scared and ran from You again.

But I never forgot all You had done or shown me. And even though I ran, there was a part of me that longed to be with You, so I ran back to You. I decided that I wanted You more than I wanted myself. Myself was just going to get me into those dark and desperate places again, and I could not take my children there.

You gave me two reasons to live: my daughters. Through them, You started to show me that I was indeed essential. It started with them, and as I grew in You, I started to see my own worth, purpose, value, and indeed identity. I was more than just their mom; I was Your child, and You wanted me. I was somehow essential to You.

As the real journey with You started, as I continue to grow in You, and as my relationship with You deepens, I see more and more worth in myself. I can now see that I have purpose and value, and that somehow I fit into the body of Christ. I look back onto that time and place, and it seems like a distant memory, almost completely faded.

Today, I am an essential part of what You are trying to do in this world, a light which is growing and shines brighter into this darkness with each day I am together with You. For me, essential is not fame or fortune; it is being a light that shines with purpose and love, and I am grateful for the love You shine on me.

~ ~ ~ ~

The Lord God is my strength; He will make my feet like deer's feet, and He will make me walk on my high hills.

—Habakkuk 3:19 (NKJV)

Let your light so shine before men, that they may see your good works and glorify your Father in heaven.

—Matthew 5:16 (NKJV)

Another parable He put forth to them, saying: "The kingdom of heaven is like a mustard seed, which a man took and sowed in his field, which indeed is the least of all the seeds; but when it is grown it is greater than the herbs and becomes a tree, so that the birds of the air come and nest in its branches."

—Matthew 13:31–32 (NKJV)

Work willingly at whatever you do, as though you were working for the Lord rather than for people.

—Colossians 3:23 (NLT)

I Am ... Family

Family. For many, it is not a safe place nor a place of fond memories. It often isn't for me, Lord. While not everything was bad, it was where I learned rejection, failure, blame, and worthlessness. I grew up being told I would never amount to anything, being treated completely different than siblings, excluded, never shown any real love, compassion, or encouragement. Yet that is where You placed me; I often wondered why.

As I grew older, it was a place I wanted to escape from, even though I longed so much to be included in it. The less love I felt, the more love I desired. The more I was told I was a failure, the more I wanted to prove I was not. Family was not a great place in my world, and in many ways, it hasn't changed. Growing up this way, and indeed still being treated this way, makes family an interesting concept for me.

As I grow up in You, as I travel this journey with You, probably the biggest lesson family is teaching me is forgiveness. It is where I harbor the most insecurity, rejection, and doubt. It is where I need to forgive the most, accept the most, and love the most. It is still a process for me at times.

All throughout Your word, You say to me, to all of us, that we are family: included and loved. But more than that even, we are heirs in Christ, we are royalty, we have You, "Abba, Father," who we can come to at any time, no matter what we have experienced from our earthly families. We actually belong to You.

You have laid out on a silver platter all the things I have ever longed for and yearned for. And while it has taken me a very long time, with a lot of prayer, purging, forgiveness, and trust, being included in Your family, as a child of God, is the highest honor and greatest privilege I will ever receive. Belonging to Your family, being Your child and knowing that I am Your child, is the difference.

Everything I feel I lacked, I have received without question from You. I can stand proudly and say that I have the best Father there ever was, is, and is to come. I have an endless, enduring, constant, and consistently faithful rock, one I would not have if I were not family. Thank You, Lord.

~ ~ ~ ~

For those who are led by the Spirit of God are the children of God. The Spirit you received does not make you slaves, so that you live in fear again; rather, the Spirit you received brought about your adoption to sonship. And by him we cry, "Abba, Father." The Spirit himself testifies with our spirit that we are God's children.

—Romans 8:14–16 (NIV)

For you are all sons of God through faith in Christ Jesus.

—Galatians 3:26 (NKJV)

But when the time arrived that was set by God the Father, God sent his Son, born among us of a woman, born under the conditions of the law so that he might redeem those of us who have been kidnapped by the law. Thus we have been set free to experience our rightful heritage. You can tell for sure that you are now fully adopted as his own children because God sent the Spirit of his Son into our lives crying out, "Papa! Father!" Doesn't that privilege of intimate conversation with God make it plain that you are not a slave, but a child? And if you are a child, you're also an heir, with complete access to the inheritance.

—Galatians 4:6–7 (MSG)

But when the kindness and the love of God our Savior toward man appeared, not by works of righteousness which we have done, but according to His mercy He saved us, through the washing of regeneration and renewing of the Holy Spirit, whom He poured out on us abundantly through Jesus Christ our Savior, that having been justified by His grace we should become heirs according to the hope of eternal life.

—Titus 3:4–7 (NKJV)

I Am ... Free

Lord, I grew up with a certain amount of religion in me. What I learned more than anything was that I am a sinner, and You have a lot of rules that I must obey; if I didn't, then I was hell-bound on a fast train.

To a degree, that wrecked my childhood. It instilled fear and then later acceptance, but acceptance in the wrong place. It wasn't enough that I endured the rejection I did, but I was actually taught that You rejected me too because I was so far from perfect.

Never, not once, was the message of Jesus told to me. Not once was I ever told that You loved me just as I was, where I was. Not once was I told that You sent Your Son to save me and set me free from all the condemnation and baggage that I carried—even as a child.

It took a very long, windy, bumpy road, filled with massive potholes and mistakes, to get to a place where I actually knew beyond a shadow of doubt that You loved me and You came to set me free.

I also learned that I have an enemy. He plants lies about You and about me. He uses anything he can, including religion, to do it (unless the message of religion includes the message of Jesus). He comes to literally and spiritually kill, steal, and destroy all that You created and all that Jesus conquered.

You came so that I could have life: real life, free life. Coming to Christ, accepting Your invitation to salvation and freedom, started to liberate me from the lies. I realized that when Jesus said on the cross, "It is finished," He actually meant that He had conquered everything that my enemy was trying to do.

When I see myself as free, when I truly walk into all that Jesus finished, a place where true freedom exists, the enemy can no longer prowl around me. Everything I have ever faced, everything I have ever endured, every fear that haunts or hinders me, every bondage I carry, was nailed at the cross with Jesus, which made me free.

Freedom in Christ is a powerful position to be in. And the more

I find that out, the more I face outside and indeed inside, the more freedom I have. Yes, I have sinned, and I continue to do stupid things and make mistakes, but I also have the freedom of knowing that I am not condemned for them, and that I am growing in freedom through them. Thank You, Jesus.

~ ~ ~ ~

Then Jesus said to those Jews who believed Him, "If you abide in My word, you are My disciples indeed. And you shall know the truth, and the truth shall make you free."

—John 8:31–32 (NKJV)

The thief does not come except to steal, and to kill, and to destroy. I have come that they may have life, and that they may have it more abundantly.

—John 10:10 (NKJV)

We are made right with God by placing our faith in Jesus Christ. And this is true for everyone who believes, no matter who we are. For everyone has sinned; we all fall short of God's glorious standard. Yet God, in his grace, freely makes us right in his sight. He did this through Christ Jesus when he freed us from the penalty for our sins.

—Romans 3:22–24 (NLT)

There is therefore now no condemnation to those who are in Christ Jesus, who do not walk according to the flesh, but according to the Spirit. For the law of the Spirit of life in Christ Jesus has made me free from the law of sin and death.

—Romans 8:1–2 (NKJV)

I Am ... Promised

From the beginning to the end, Your word, the Bible, is filled with Your promises. One promise that You have always kept is giving us, Your awesome creation, the free will to choose and decide for ourselves what we are going to do.

Yet You don't leave us there, in the dark, confused, and blind. You give us instruction, choices, and consequences. You lay it all out as clear as day. You put life and death before us and then actually tell us to choose life, to choose You.

You know way more than we do what will happen if we don't, and still You give us the freedom to find out for ourselves. That is so awesome.

That in itself shows what an unselfish God You really are. Before there were any kind of rules, Lord, You showed love and a desire to have a relationship with us. You created us to have a relationship with You, yet You gave us the choice whether we wanted to have one with You. So good. So gracious.

Throughout history, throughout my own life, You have given choices, and each one has a consequence: good or bad. You leave me to choose what it is I want, what I desire, where I want to be.

For so long, I chose to camp out in a desert place, yet You were still with me, as promised. When I rebelled against You, my parents, and indeed myself, You were still there, promising me a better life and a future, if I would just change camps. When things looked darkest, You sent Your one and only Son, not to condemn me but to save me. You promised me a way out, and You provided one.

No matter where I am and no matter what I am going through, You have a promise for me that fits that exact place and time. You have never failed to deliver on a single promise, Lord, and I don't believe You ever will.

You have shown me time after time that You are faithful and true to Your word. You do not lie. You do not promise things and then not deliver on them. You know perfectly what we all need, at the exact time we need it, and the exact place we need it.

You are faithful, and I am guaranteed everything You ever promised me: freedom, protection, a way out, guidance, relationship, hope, peace, joy, goodness, love, faithfulness, and indeed a future: a good, great, honest future, a future with You and all that You desire for me. What an amazing promise to have.

~ ~ ~ ~

Today I have given you the choice between life and death, between blessings and curses. Now I call on heaven and earth to witness the choice you make. Oh, that you would choose life, so that you and your descendants might live!

—Deuteronomy 30:19 (NLT)

Let us hold fast the confession of our hope without wavering, for He who promised is faithful.

—Hebrews 10:23 (NKJV)

This truth gives them confidence that they have eternal life, which God—who does not lie—promised them before the world began.

—Titus 1:2 (NLT)

And because of his glory and excellence, he has given us great and precious promises. These are the promises that enable you to share his divine nature and escape the world's corruption caused by human desires.

—2 Peter 1:4 (NLT)

And this is the promise that He has promised us—eternal life.

—1 John 2:25 (NKJV)

I Am ... Secure

For some reason, I think that as we grow older, we become more fearful and insecure. No matter what we grew up with, I think we live in one of two camps: reckless, without consideration for ourselves and others, or so incredibly secure, no one can penetrate our safeness.

When it comes to You, and the real security we can find in and with You, we are either afraid of offending others at the mention of Jesus, or we just march right in and blast others for not following You.

I've been in that camp, where I just accept the world for what it is and didn't want to talk about You, for fear of the reaction I might receive, and now I'm sitting here writing, wanting the whole world to know about You (without hitting them over the head, of course).

I don't know where my line in the sand was washed away nor when it all changed, but I think it was when I really started to see me in You and You in me.

It's a personal journey for each of us, yet we are so interconnected to each other and to You. I get how we need to be aware, on guard, smart, and wise with our decisions, yet the best decision I ever made was to put my faith and trust in You. When I trust in You and place my faith in You, I know without a doubt that I am secure. I know that no matter what happens, You have my situation in Your control.

I used to ask "Why?" to everything; now, I ask either "What?" or "How?" What are You trying to show me or teach me, Lord? How do You want to use me here, Lord? My security in You has led to growth and purpose. My security in You has reduced my fears and eliminated my insecurities. You have placed an eternal seal on my life. You shield me from danger. You fight my battles. You empower me, and I have Holy Spirit. What do I have to be afraid of?

I can never outgive You, I can never do too much good or be too caring, and I certainly cannot run out of love. With You, my world gets bigger and bigger. With You, I am secure.

~ ~ ~ ~

As for God, His way is perfect; the word of the Lord is proven; He is a shield to all who trust in Him.

—Psalm 18:30 (NKJV)

He will cover you with his feathers. He will shelter you with his wings. His faithful promises are your armor and protection.

—Psalm 91:4 (NLT)

Now it is God who establishes and confirms us in joint fellowship with you in Christ, and who has anointed us empowering us with the gifts of the Spirit; it is He who has also put His seal on us that is, He has appropriated us and certified us as His and has given us the Holy Spirit in our hearts as a pledge like a security deposit to guarantee the fulfillment of His promise of eternal life.

—2 Corinthians 1:21–22 (AMP)

And you also were included in Christ when you heard the message of truth, the gospel of your salvation. When you believed, you were marked in him with a seal, the promised Holy Spirit, who is a deposit guaranteeing our inheritance until the redemption of those who are God's possession—to the praise of his glory.

—Ephesians 1:13–14 (NIV)

Lord Jesus, May the precious person reading this book feel the presence of your Holy Spirit. May this reader find You and Your unconditional love. May they know who You are and fully understand the lengths that You have gone in order to reach their heart and touch their life. May they understand Your grace and know that it covers every hurt or regret they have. You are an amazing, life-changing, healing God, and I ask this in your powerful name. Amen.

—Andrea M., nineteen years
clean and sober, by God's
amazing grace

PART 3

I Am ... Alive

I am alive. Like, really alive. I have new air in my lungs, new blood in my veins, and a new spirit throughout my whole being. Your grace has reached me, Lord, and I am so grateful. You have taken me from death and destruction (my own self-willed destruction, the destructive patterns of my past, my upbringing, generational destruction) to newness of life, a life with You, a life of You.

You gave Yourself to me: the most amazing gift I could have ever received because it is everlasting. You never run out on me, You are always with me, and You accepted me as I was, with all my brokenness and the baggage I carried. You took it from me—all that stuff I carried around with me, some I wasn't even aware of.

I didn't have to jump through hoops. I didn't have to be perfect. In fact, that's how You wanted me, so You could show me that Your mercy and grace can indeed reach the unexplainable depths of despair.

Lord, I am so grateful for the grace You have shown me; You not only forgive me of everything from my past, You also forgive anything I might do. You still don't expect perfection from me. You just want me to live with You and learn through this awesome Spirit You have given me so freely. I don't have to carry stuff with me anymore. I can just bring it to You and lay it down at the cross. I just "Let go and let God" now.

You have changed everything and have given me a reason to live, and by that, I feel so incredibly alive. Thank You so much, Jesus. I want to live like I am truly alive now.

~ ~ ~ ~

For since by man came death, by Man also came the resurrection of the dead. For as in Adam all die, even so in Christ all shall be made alive.
—1 Corinthians 15:21–22 (NKJV)

For when I tried to keep the law, it condemned me. So I died to the law—I stopped trying to meet all its requirements—so that I might live for God. My old self has been crucified with Christ. It is no longer I who live, but Christ lives in me. So I live in this earthly body by trusting in the Son of God, who loved me and gave himself for me.

—Galatians 2:19–20 (NLT)

But because of his great love for us, God, who is rich in mercy, made us alive with Christ even when we were dead in transgressions—it is by grace you have been saved. And God raised us up with Christ and seated us with him in the heavenly realms in Christ Jesus, in order that in the coming ages he might show the incomparable riches of his grace, expressed in his kindness to us in Christ Jesus.

—Ephesians 2:4–7 (NIV)

And you, being dead in your trespasses and the uncircumcision of your flesh, He has made alive together with Him, having forgiven you all trespasses, having wiped out the handwriting of requirements that was against us, which was contrary to us. And He has taken it out of the way, having nailed it to the cross.

—Colossians 2:13–14 (NKJV)

I Am ... Called

How long have I strived within my own power and strength to achieve anything in this life? The amount of time that I can look back on as utterly wasted is amazing. What I am so grateful for, Lord, is that nothing, not one single thing, is ever wasted in Your eyes.

It really doesn't matter where we have come from: addiction, desperation, depression, abused or abusive, manipulated or manipulative: I could go on and on. You waste none of it. You turn it all around for those who love You, and You actually use it to promote Your kingdom. You call us all to something and then clothe us in Yourself, Your power, Your word, and Your Spirit to make it all possible.

I am called, as Your masterpiece, to walk in the fullness of the destiny You have prepared for me. Not halfway or partway but in the true fullness of what You have planned: freely, gently, humbly, lovingly, and peacefully. That is what I have been called to do; that is what we have all been called to do.

I have a part to play. I have been included in Your master plan. I am vital and called to make a difference. I have been called to live in the amazing and complete freedom that living with You brings.

Based on my past, the things I have been through and the things I have done, I really don't deserve any of the amazing things that living with You brings, but that is what living with You and being called by You brings: blessing, redemption, togetherness, inclusion, freedom, and indeed love.

Oh, Your love, Lord: The grace and mercy You have showered on me. I used to wonder if I would ever make it through so many of the hard times, hard times and trials both with You and without you.

Trials are going to come; life is indeed not perfect in this world, and it isn't fair. But life with You is far better than without You. Somehow, the things I am called to be, and indeed go through, grow me and grow me into the perfection You designed me to be. You planned it all out, even what I consider hardship or failure. You planned it for me because You wanted to use it for what You called me to do.

It is not wasted; it is not unworthy. It is part of my journey, and through it all, I am blessed to be called by You.

~ ~ ~ ~

For you, brethren, have been called to liberty; only do not use liberty as an opportunity for the flesh, but through love serve one another.

—Galatians 5:13 (NKJV)

Therefore I, a prisoner for serving the Lord, beg you to lead a life worthy of your calling, for you have been called by God. Always be humble and gentle. Be patient with each other, making allowance for each other's faults because of your love. Make every effort to keep yourselves united in the Spirit, binding yourselves together with peace. For there is one body and one Spirit, just as you have been called to one glorious hope for the future.

—Ephesians 4:1–4 (NLT)

For God saved us and called us to live a holy life. He did this, not because we deserved it, but because that was his plan from before the beginning of time—to show us his grace through Christ Jesus. And now he has made all of this plain to us by the appearing of Christ Jesus, our Savior. He broke the power of death and illuminated the way to life and immortality through the Good News.

—2 Timothy 1:9–10 (NLT)

Finally, all of you be of one mind, having compassion for one another; love as brothers, be tenderhearted, be courteous; not returning evil for evil or reviling for reviling, but on the contrary blessing, knowing that you were called to this, that you may inherit a blessing.

—1 Peter 3:8–9 (NKJV)

I Am ... Comforted

Failure, depression, the unhealthy labels I wore: Only a few times in my childhood did I ever feel any comfort or true reprieve from them. I looked for comfort, or perhaps escape, in all the wrong places because where I thought they should be coming from, they weren't.

I don't know what really led me to You all those many years ago, but something did, and I accepted Your love for me as a teen. But then, of course, without really knowing anything much about You (or indeed myself), I wandered off Your path into yet deeper and darker places, still seeking that comfort and love.

It was when I experienced an incredible loss in my life that I came running back to You. At times it was a sprint, and at times it was a "Hang on, what if ..." But I have found, Lord, that You are indeed the master comforter. No matter what I face, no matter what I lose, no matter how hurt I am, You are there. You lift me up, and You have put others around me to do the same, in a good way, in a truly loving and compassionate way.

There are times when I feel comfort can come only from You, and it is only You I want to go to for that; other times, it can come from the amazing family You have placed around me. Sometimes, You are just silent and let me talk it all out to You; other times, I will feel my spirit being moved by You into a safe and healing place. You have blessed me with the feelings of loss and remembrance and shown me purpose through it all.

You have blessed me with a Spirit inside me, connected to me, a beacon of hope that shines like a lighthouse, lighting my way. Sometimes, I need comforting over my own poor decisions, and sometimes, it's just because of life. But You are always there, never judging me and like a warm hug, a hot cup of tea, or just a peaceful feeling that creeps into my soul, telling me that everything is okay and there is nothing I can't face, even this.

I am indeed comforted, but now it is from all the right places, and through my losses and my gains, my gains through You, rather than the hindrances of my past, that I am able to be of help to others.

~ ~ ~ ~

The Lord is close to the brokenhearted and saves those who are crushed in spirit. The righteous person may have many troubles, but the Lord delivers him from them all; he protects all his bones, not one of them will be broken.

—Psalm 34:18–20 (NIV)

You're blessed when you feel you've lost what is most dear to you. Only then can you be embraced by the One most dear to you.

—Matthew 5:4 (MSG)

If you love me, show it by doing what I've told you. I will talk to the Father, and he'll provide you another Friend so that you will always have someone with you. This Friend is the Spirit of Truth. The godless world can't take him in because it doesn't have eyes to see him, doesn't know what to look for. But you know him already because he has been staying with you, and will even be in you!

—John 14:15–17 (MSG)

Praise be to the God and Father of our Lord Jesus Christ, the Father of compassion and the God of all comfort, who comforts us in all our troubles, so that we can comfort those in any trouble with the comfort we ourselves receive from God.

—2 Corinthians 1:3–4 (NIV)

If you've gotten anything at all out of following Christ, if his love has made any difference in your life, if being in a community of the Spirit means anything to you, if you have a heart, if you care—then do me a favor: Agree with each other, love each other, be deep-spirited friends. Don't push your way to the front; don't sweet-talk your way to the top. Put yourself aside, and help others get ahead. Don't be obsessed with getting your own advantage. Forget yourselves long enough to lend a helping hand.

—Philippians 2:1–4 (MSG)

I Am ... Empowered

Your power has stamped all the "ick" out of my life. You have done it. You have done what I could never do, in spite of my best efforts. When I was at my weakest, You gave me strength to overcome things that I have been battling for years. And while I'm not perfect yet, I press in to You because I know I cannot do any of this with my own will.

I bring my things, my issues, my hopes, my dreams, and I give them to You, and You do the rest. That is so incredibly empowering for me. You give freedom in this great love of Yours.

I feel my spirit dancing within me with this amazing power; I feel like I could conquer my part of this world with You beside me and inside of me. I feel so renewed and refreshed. I sleep better, even soundly, like I have no worries at all.

Obviously, there are things and people I care deeply about, but I pray to You, give it all to You, and You guide me. You give me rest. You give me inner peace. You give me strength. You give me hope. You give me love. You give me guidance; there are things I don't want to do anymore because they don't line up with what is actually right; while I'm far from perfect, You just accept my progress and cheer me on.

There are times when I feel in my own spirit that thousands of angels are cheering me on, and that is so encouraging and empowering, especially when worldly life still goes on around me. I know that I can do things, things that give me purpose and meaning, with Your Spirit and strength inside of me.

As I grow in You, as I learn more about You, I learn more about me and am empowered by it all even more. It is truly an amazing experience living with You. Thank You, Jesus. I am so grateful for Your encouragement and empowerment.

~ ~ ~ ~

He gives power to the weak, and to those who have no might He increases strength. Even the youths shall faint and be weary, and the young men shall utterly fall, but those who wait on the Lord shall renew their strength; they shall mount up with wings like eagles, they shall run and not be weary, they shall walk and not faint.

—Isaiah 40:29–31 (NKJV)

But he who is joined to the Lord is one spirit with Him.

—1 Corinthians 6:17 (NKJV)

Now He who provides seed for the sower and bread for food will provide and multiply your seed for sowing that is, your resources and increase the harvest of your righteousness which shows itself in active goodness, kindness, and love.

—2 Corinthians 9:10 (AMP)

And may you have the power to understand, as all God's people should, how wide, how long, how high, and how deep his love is. May you experience the love of Christ, though it is too great to understand fully. Then you will be made complete with all the fullness of life and power that comes from God.

—Ephesians 3:18–19 (NLT)

And my God shall supply all your need according to His riches in glory by Christ Jesus.

—Philippians 4:19 (NKJV)

I AM ... FOUND

People often look at us and say so glibly that we found God, but the truth is that Your pursuit of us is far greater than our ability to wander (or indeed run) from You. You are relentless in Your pursuit to find us and to let us know that we have indeed been found.

Being found is the most liberating experience. Life with You has turned my life around. I look back and can see just how much I needed You, yet just how much of my pride kept me from You. Time after time, You would show me things, and time after time, I was so arrogant and prideful, like I was somehow god of my life and did not need You. Even in my lost-ness, my pride was still very much intact. I can do it. I can make it. I don't need You: Those kinds of attitudes keep us away from You.

Another thing is fear. Oh, the fear of actually submitting to this God, who is going to demand this and that, who wants nothing except perfection, and if I falter, He will send me straight to hell. Such lies the enemy tells us about You. But that is so not who You are nor what You are about.

You seek Your children. You pursue us with love. You want to bless us with amazing, thriving lives. You want to take us out of darkness and indeed pluck us from the clutches of hell itself, redeeming us into Your kingdom. You are so incredibly caring to me and to us all. You only want to give me the very, very best and actually ask for so little from me. You give me everything I could possibly need to lead a prosperous life with You. I'm never alone. I am always guided. I'm allowed to make mistakes and have Your grace and forgiveness covering me all the time.

I am so grateful to be on this side of life now, Lord. You have shown me thousands of times how many lies I have been told about You. You haven't told me; You have shown me.

My enemy just tells me lies and tries to keep me trapped back there, without hope, love, or forgiveness. But You show me love. You show me forgiveness. You show me hope, grace, a future, and You celebrate with me in all the small victories I make.

Thank You, Lord, for finding me. In You and with You, I am found in so many ways: emotionally, spiritually, mentally. Each step of the way, as more layers are revealed and as I walk with You, the more I find and the more found I am. Bless You, Lord. I am so grateful.

~ ~ ~ ~

Suppose one of you had a hundred sheep and lost one. Wouldn't you leave the ninety-nine in the wilderness and go after the lost one until you found it? When found, you can be sure you would put it across your shoulders, rejoicing, and when you got home call in your friends and neighbors, saying, "Celebrate with me! I've found my lost sheep!" Count on it—there's more joy in heaven over one sinner's rescued life than over ninety-nine good people in no need of rescue.

—Luke 15:6–7 (MSG)

Or imagine a woman who has ten coins and loses one. Won't she light a lamp and scour the house, looking in every nook and cranny until she finds it? And when she finds it you can be sure she'll call her friends and neighbors: "Celebrate with me! I found my lost coin!" Count on it—that's the kind of party God's angels throw every time one lost soul turns to God.

—Luke 15:9–10 (MSG)

But the father wasn't listening. He was calling to the servants, "Quick. Bring a clean set of clothes and dress him. Put the family ring on his finger and sandals on his feet. Then get a grain-fed heifer and roast it. We're going to feast! We're going to have a wonderful time! My son is here—given up for dead and now alive! Given up for lost and now found!" And they began to have a wonderful time.

—Luke 15:24 (MSG)

I Am ... A Friend

I am Your friend. Goodness, that's quite a lot to take in, just in that one tiny statement. You actually see me as Your friend. That is how close You want to be to me.

Friends have a relationship with one another. I've had many friends in my life, Lord; some were really amazing, and some were not. I've been an amazing friend to some, and I too have been that disastrous "friend." It's been a journey of trying to figure out who to trust and have in the inner circle and indeed being trustworthy of being in that inner circle of someone else.

It's been a difficult road for me. From childhood, I endured so much bullying, and as a teen, I was in a band of misfits who somehow fit together in our own misery and rebellion. As an adult, I have found that we often act and react as we were raised; for a lot of us, those were not ideal examples.

Manipulation, triangulation, who could get what from who and for how long, trying to fit square pegs into round holes, trying to find that place where I belonged, where I was accepted for who I was and not what I had (or didn't have): sad and defeating merry-go-rounds that left more hurt than joy.

It is such a refreshing breath of fresh air to know that You just accept me as I am, without wanting anything from me, except me. You want me to be the best me I can be and the me You designed me to be, and that's good, great, and even glorious. You see a diamond in the rough, and with each step of our relationship, our friendship, You are polishing me into someone better and better.

You saw hope in me when I had none. You saw someone You wanted; in fact, You saw someone You deeply desired to have a friendship with. You see my heart, and I am seeing Yours.

You speak to me as a friend, not as a controlling or manipulating God, and You speak of goodness, and righteousness, and peace. You lift me up and seat me at the head of the table instead of making me sit in a place of shame. You really do consider me Your friend.

~ ~ ~ ~

And God spoke with Moses face-to-face, as neighbors speak to one another. When he would return to the camp, his attendant, the young man Joshua, stayed—he didn't leave the Tent.

—Exodus 33:11 (MSG)

A perverse person stirs up conflict, and a gossip separates close friends.

—Proverbs 16:28 (NIV)

Whoever loves a pure heart and gracious speech will have the king as a friend.

—Proverbs 22:11 (NLT)

When you're invited to dinner, go and sit at the last place. Then when the host comes he may very well say, "Friend, come up to the front." That will give the dinner guests something to talk about! What I'm saying is, If you walk around with your nose in the air, you're going to end up flat on your face. But if you're content to be simply yourself, you will become more than yourself.

—Luke 14:10–11 (MSG)

I no longer call you servants, because a servant does not know his master's business. Instead, I have called you friends, for everything that I learned from my Father I have made known to you.

—John 15:15 (NIV)

I Am ... Receiving

There is no doubt, Lord, that I am far more comfortable being a giver than a receiver. I don't exactly know where that mindset comes from; probably from having a lack of self-worth and value for so many years. But I am learning, Lord.

I am learning to receive all that You have for me, all that You want to bless me with, and indeed all that You have promised to me. It's vast. It is huge. It is far more than my mind can comprehend and certainly something that You are still working on within my heart.

I think I feel that I almost owe You something for whatever it is I receive from You. Yet I don't. That's just not how You are nor how You operate.

You actually want me to receive, from my salvation through Your Son Jesus, to eternity with You in heaven, and everything in between. It is actually through Your giving to me that I am healed: healed of everything in my mind, body, soul, and spirit.

You always work from the inside out, and the sooner I actually grasp this with true belief and knowledge, the sooner I will be healed of it all. Sometimes, I don't understand why I am still in awe of what You do for me; I can actually get a condemning voice in my head that says I don't believe or I have somehow failed You, yet You come through in spite of me. I know those voices aren't from You, Lord, because You just love me and want to encourage me, not condemn me.

But I can say this, Lord: When that voice does come, I am now able to kick it out, and it actually spurs me on, triumphant in calling Satan a liar and walking more boldly into what You are wanting to bless me with. I'm starting to beat him at his own game. And that I will gratefully receive from You.

There is one thing I would like to ask, Lord: As my belief continues to get stronger with each breath and step, and as I continue to receive more, without obligation or ulterior motive, without any requirement or contract from You, please help me receive with more grace.

I know that You will, Lord, because You are faithful, and I am receiving.

~ ~ ~ ~

You intended to harm me, but God intended it all for good. He brought me to this position so I could save the lives of many people.
—Genesis 50:20 (NLT)

For everyone who asks receives; the one who seeks finds; and to the one who knocks, the door will be opened.
—Matthew 7:8–11 (NIV)

Jesus said to him, "You say to Me, 'If You can?' All things are possible for the one who believes and trusts in Me!" Immediately the father of the boy cried out with a desperate, piercing cry, saying, "I do believe; help me overcome my unbelief."
—Mark 9:23–24 (AMP)

Then the King will say to those on his right, "Come, you who are blessed by my Father; take your inheritance, the kingdom prepared for you since the creation of the world."
—Matthew 25:34 (NIV)

Without becoming weak in faith he considered his own body, now as good as dead for producing children since he was about a hundred years old, and he considered the deadness of Sarah's womb. But he did not doubt or waver in unbelief concerning the promise of God, but he grew strong and empowered by faith, giving glory to God, being fully convinced that God had the power to do what He had promised.
—Romans 4:19–21 (AMP)

I Am ... Renewed

It's really so incredibly simple, Lord, and I am so grateful for that. You don't make me "work" for anything. There are no hoops to jump through or targets to hit. You seem to just do it all. All it takes from me is time with You, and that is just so cool. I can have a song in my head all day, and that can be enough. I can spend time just thinking about something I read or heard, and that can be enough. It seems to me that my relationship with You is what really counts. And even that, You make really easy.

I don't have to understand everything, and I can ask questions without being condemned or feeling dumb or stupid. There seems to be this natural, innate flow between You and me, that just renews everything through relationship and time. Time with You gives me new energy, new strength, new thoughts, new wisdom.

I understand more and more as time goes on and as things happen in this world and, indeed, to or with me. You give me the ability to distinguish what is from You and what isn't. My brain and my emotions can be my worst enemies, and thoughts that blame, condemn, shame, or ridicule me can still float up in there. But I know they aren't from You.

I understand that there is an enemy who doesn't want me to succeed or even progress, so I am able to hold on to what You say and kick the garbage of my mind out to the curb. And the more I do that, the more I'm actually able to do that. But it's effortless, really. It's just from spending time with You in whatever way that looks like: listening to music, reading Your word, hearing messages, or being around other believers.

I'm being transformed from the inside out, and even when my outside world doesn't seem to change much, my inner world sure is. And with that renewal inside, I have this amazing inner strength from You that helps me deal with outside and actually speaks life into the outside.

Jesus, I'm really grateful for the simplicity of it all. I'm grateful that You sent Holy Spirit to live in everyone who comes to You. I'm grateful that He is my light and works for my renewal. I am so blessed.

~ ~ ~ ~

But those who wait on the Lord shall renew their strength; they shall mount up with wings like eagles, they shall run and not be weary, they shall walk and not faint.

—Isaiah 40:31 (NKJV)

Do not conform to the pattern of this world, but be transformed by the renewing of your mind. Then you will be able to test and approve what God's will is—his good, pleasing and perfect will.

—Romans 12:2 (NIV)

We demolish arguments and every pretension that sets itself up against the knowledge of God, and we take captive every thought to make it obedient to Christ.

—2 Corinthians 10:5 (NIV)

Instead, let the Spirit renew your thoughts and attitudes. Put on your new nature, created to be like God—truly righteous and holy.

—Ephesians 4:23–24 (NLT)

Put on your new nature, and be renewed as you learn to know your Creator and become like him.

—Colossians 3:10 (NLT)

Father, in the Name of Jesus, I pray that in the same way You have forgiven me, help me to forgive those who have hurt or mistreated me. I pray that You would restore my soul and the souls of my family, and reconcile our relationships with one another; that they will be better, healthier, and more loving than before. I thank You that I see myself and others through Your eyes, that I grow in the knowledge of who I am and whose I am. In Jesus' name, Amen.

Marvin and Jacquie McGee
Pastors
Relate Church, Canada

PART 4

I Am ... Anointed and Appointed

When I sink into You, You ignite something inside me and invite me to partner with You and what You are doing. You only ever lead with love, never guilt, shame, or fear. You enable and empower all those You are raising up. And that includes me.

You have all authority; You have anointed and established me to pursue hope and freedom. Lord, You know that I used to be so lost and so afraid. You know everything about me, and You still considered me worthy of walking with You.

You have given to me and sealed me with Your Spirit; each and every day, You minister to me, helping me overcome and helping me to help others overcome. I was one of those oppressed and blind people You have freed, and I will proclaim Your glory. Lord, You have raised up so many incredibly broken people.

Some of my favorite people are those who weren't raised in the church, but those who came from the deepest, darkest places: depression, addiction, despair. They seem more real, I guess (or at least I can relate to them better). They don't have an air of perfection about them. they have an air of redemption and of You. They project more Jesus, maybe? And yet hearing their testimonies, and the fact that they have been anointed and appointed by You, it seems to just encourage me in my journey and helps me to know that I too have been anointed and appointed by You.

I love that no matter what we have done, You have a purpose for it and a special calling for each one of us, something that only we can bring to the table: your banquet table, the place where the whole body comes together to celebrate and glorify all that You have ever done and all that You will ever do.

Your way is so simple, Lord. When we truly experience the freedom of our purpose and identity with You, there is such incredible simplicity to all. It's not complicated or confusing.

We are so blessed to have Holy Spirit with us, unwinding all that we have wound up and unbinding all the bondage we have made. I just get to walk forward with You. Sounds pretty simple to me. Thank You, Jesus!

~ ~ ~ ~

I will raise up for myself a faithful priest, who will do according to what is in my heart and mind. I will firmly establish his priestly house, and they will minister before my anointed one always.

—1 Samuel 2:35 (NIV)

The Spirit of the Lord is on me, because he has anointed me to proclaim good news to the poor. He has sent me to proclaim freedom for the prisoners and recovery of sight for the blind, to set the oppressed free, to proclaim the year of the Lord's favor.

—Luke 4:18–19 (NIV)

Now He who establishes us with you in Christ and has anointed us is God, who also has sealed us and given us the Spirit in our hearts as a guarantee.

—2 Corinthians 1:21–22 (NKJV)

We, however, will not boast beyond measure, but within the limits of the sphere which God appointed us—a sphere which especially includes you.

—2 Corinthians 10:13 (NKJV)

I Am ... Believing

I think we are all born with the ability to believe in something greater than ourselves. There is this beacon of hope in all our circumstances that keeps us pushing forward ... somehow.

When I was at my lowest, when I missed the abuse I had been enduring; when I was ridden with guilt, shame, and condemnation; when I felt utter rejection from those I thought should have been the most caring in my life; when I felt completely lost and totally alone, there was something that told me to keep going and keep trying.

Today, I know that was Your voice and Your Spirit. Just like Holy Spirit was there before time, hovering over empty space, He was there, hovering over me, waiting to be spoken into action.

Whatever I believe, that is what I am and will become. It took a whole lot of self-imposed heartache to actually believe that You were real, Lord. It took brokenness and wanting something better. It took believing that there was something, anything, good about me and about this world to bring me to You.

Since coming to You and accepting Your invitation, I have discovered one very cool thing: My ability to believe will never catch up to Your ability to perform; it just isn't possible. What I see and what I believe are but a speck on an artist's canvas. You are the master painter, somehow painting this great landscape called my life.

Your power did not stop at the cross, nor did it stop after I was saved. It is still very much alive today. Your power is transforming me and purging me and making me new. I know this because I experience it. I know this because I feel it. But it all started with believing. Each day, as I experience more, I believe more. I may not be able to see You outside of myself, but I see you inside.

You are taking me to amazing places. It is through reaching up to You and saying "Lord" that I believe. It is through bending down in heartache and crying "Lord" that I believe. I came to You by faith, and faith by believing; that's all it took. And that's all it ever will take: believing.

~ ~ ~ ~

Jesus said to him, "Thomas, because you have seen Me, you have believed. Blessed are those who have not seen and yet have believed."

—John 20:29 (NKJV)

All the prophets testify about Him, that through His name everyone who believes in Him whoever trusts in and relies on Him, accepting Him as Savior and Messiah receives forgiveness of sins.

—Acts 10:43 (AMP)

It's news I'm most proud to proclaim, this extraordinary Message of God's powerful plan to rescue everyone who trusts him, starting with Jews and then right on to everyone else! God's way of putting people right shows up in the acts of faith, confirming what Scripture has said all along: "The person in right standing before God by trusting him really lives."

—Romans 1:16–17 (MSG)

It was by faith that Rahab the prostitute was not destroyed with the people in her city who refused to obey God. For she had given a friendly welcome to the spies.

—Hebrews 11:31 (NLT)

God chose him as your ransom long before the world began, but now in these last days he has been revealed for your sake. Through Christ you have come to trust in God. And you have placed your faith and hope in God because he raised Christ from the dead and gave him great glory.

—1 Peter 1:20–21 (NLT)

I Am ... Blessed

You abundantly bless me, Lord, far greater than I could have ever imagined. Not only through saving me from my own self and destruction, but in everyday things. It seems like the more faithful I am in trusting You, the more You shower blessings on me, so I trust more and am blessed more. You never run out.

You bless me with love around me, something I have always craved and chased. And I don't have to chase it anymore; it's right here, and You gave it to me.

You bless me with comfort when I'm down; I don't need to go dump my issues or my worries onto anyone else. I just dump them on You; You actually listen, and if I'm quiet long enough, You give the answer through my spirit.

Outwardly, You have blessed me, but only so that I can in turn be a blessing to others. Whatever I am given, I need to give back. And when I give, I too am blessed.

Your goodness isn't just by invitation but by encounter. You have blessed me with daily encounters with You, because no matter what my day holds, no matter what happens outside, what really matters is what happens inside; that is where You really are: inside.

You are within me, blessing my spirit and lining my life up with Your vision of it, so that I can be that blessing You always wanted me to be, a blessing not only to myself, but also to those around me, and indeed blessing You by being the me you designed me to be.

You are so incredibly gracious with how You deal with me. And in all things, my past, my present, my future, my old, my new, my broken, my repaired, my ugly, and my beautiful, I am indeed blessed through it all.

Your ways, Lord, are so much higher than ours that it is really hard for me to comprehend them. And certainly as a baby, I couldn't. But as I grow, as the scales are removed from both my eyes and my heart, I see much more clearly all that You intended.

Your beauty is everywhere I look, including inside of me. Thank You, Lord, for blessing me so much more than I can ever try to thank You for.

~ ~ ~ ~

Blessed is he who considers the poor; the Lord will deliver him in time of trouble.

—Psalm 41:1 (NKJV)

Happy are those who hear the joyful call to worship, for they will walk in the light of your presence, Lord.

—Psalm 89:15 (NLT)

Blessed is the man who trusts in the Lord, and whose hope is the Lord.

—Jeremiah 17:7 (NKJV)

Oh, what joy for those whose disobedience is forgiven, whose sins are put out of sight. Yes, what joy for those whose record the Lord has cleared of sin.

—Romans 4:7–8 (NLT)

But whoever looks intently into the perfect law that gives freedom, and continues in it—not forgetting what they have heard, but doing it—they will be blessed in what they do.

—James 1:25 (NIV)

I AM ... FEARLESS

I have lived in fear and from a place of fear. I have dreaded what others might think or say. I have lived a life trying to please the unpleasable people. I have settled for abuse, not knowing I was worth more and afraid of being alone. I have lived in fear of being rejected beyond what I had already endured. I have lived in fear of being abandoned, by anyone. Fear was my life, and I didn't even know it.

But You, Lord, make me fearless to share my story, my testimony of living with You. You make me fearless to share, to make a difference, to unlock someone else's prison. It's a humbling experience, Lord, because it's raw, and it's real, and it's opening up areas of my life and exposing them. But it's about You and what You are doing in me.

You give me the courage. You give me the wisdom, and I trust in You. You have told me to be strong and of good courage. Your word says more than any other command given: "Do not fear." You take up my battles. You shelter me. You go before me. You guide me. You give me Your power to conquer anything I face. You never leave me, and You do not abandon me.

When unexpected things come, and my innate instinct is to turn to worry or fear, I am learning to trust You, and through that, I do not fear. With You, I am like David up against Goliath, using Your name and cutting off the heads of evil spirits, temptations, and things that want to overpower or scare me.

There is no need to fear with You, Lord, because You are my solid foundation. You have always delivered on every promise made. You are faithful, and You are with me. You are more powerful than any enemy who comes against me and any situation I face. Your perfect love gets rid of all my fear.

~ ~ ~ ~

Be strong and of good courage, do not fear nor be afraid of them; for the Lord your God, He is the One who goes with you. He will not leave you nor forsake you.

—Deuteronomy 31:6 (NKJV)

You will not have to fight this battle. Take up your positions; stand firm and see the deliverance the Lord will give you, Judah and Jerusalem. Do not be afraid; do not be discouraged. Go out to face them tomorrow, and the Lord will be with you.

—2 Chronicles 20:17 (NIV)

I praise God for what he has promised. I trust in God, so why should I be afraid? What can mere mortals do to me?

—Psalm 56:4 (NLT)

But whoever listens to me (Wisdom) will live securely and in confident trust and will be at ease, without fear or dread of evil.

—Proverbs 1:33 (AMP)

For God has not given us a spirit of fear, but of power and of love and of a sound mind.

—2 Timothy 1:7 (NKJV)

There is no fear in love; but perfect love casts out fear, because fear involves torment. But he who fears has not been made perfect in love.

—1 John 4:18 (NKJV)

I Am ... Growing

When it comes to growth and change, I think we are scared, because growth means change, and change means growth, and either way, it's an unknown; as we get older, the unknown becomes more fearful.

Sitting in my little self-built, self-imposed prison with the cell door wide open is more comfortable than either growth or change; it somehow feels safer than facing the unknown. Yet once I actually take those steps and get outside of that prison cell, it can be hard to wait to be grown; I want it now.

I live in such an instantaneous world. Instant information at my fingertips means no more trips to a library to look something up. Instant coffee, instant pudding, even five-minute noodles seem to take too long. It's like when babies see something they really want but aren't sure how to get over there to get it. Growing has its pains.

I have learned that it is worth it and that growing is indeed good. If I didn't grow in any way, I would still literally be a baby. And I have to grow—inside and outside—spiritually, mentally, emotionally, and physically. Life is all about growing. Even with You, Lord, growing can be hard, and it can be messy, but growth with You is just exceedingly glorious.

As I achieve each little milestone, from crawling to walking to running to resting, You are this amazing Father who is cheering me on. So incredible.

Your love breaks off all the sorrow, regret, hurt, and fears I ever felt about myself and fills those places with peace, love, and joy. You feed me what I need for each place that I am in: soft food for my baby-like faith, and as I grow, there is meat to chew on and mull over. You never expect perfection from me, and even when I am trapped in that perfection or comparison place, You correct me, train me, and get me back on track. You only want me to keep growing with You, moving forward, step by step, day by day. Forward momentum is growth.

My growth isn't a race, and I don't need to break any speed records. I just need to keep moving towards You, and You help me each step of the way as I continually look to You. I pray that You will continue to reveal Your wisdom so that my life will lead to Your plans, and Your purpose through me will come to pass as I grow.

~ ~ ~ ~

The Lord will guide you continually, and satisfy your soul in drought, and strengthen your bones; you shall be like a watered garden, and like a spring of water, whose waters do not fail.

—Isaiah 58:11 (NKJV)

Call to me and I will answer you and tell you great and unsearchable things you do not know.

—Jeremiah 33:3 (NIV)

But the Helper, the Holy Spirit, whom the Father will send in My name, He will teach you all things, and bring to your remembrance all things that I said to you.

—John 14:26 (NKJV)

For everything that was written in the past was written to teach us, so that through the endurance taught in the Scriptures and the encouragement they provide we might have hope.

—Romans 15:4 (NIV)

All Scripture is inspired by God and is useful to teach us what is true and to make us realize what is wrong in our lives. It corrects us when we are wrong and teaches us to do what is right. God uses it to prepare and equip his people to do every good work.

—2 Timothy 3:16–17 (NLT)

I Am ... Powerful

Because of my past, my upbringing, my youth, and my history, my own mind can be my greatest battlefield. It's where thoughts creep in and memories come to life. It's where the enemy attacks me the most. Today, I have more choices and even more right thinking.

When the enemy comes knocking, I have the power to not answer the door. When he tries to come through a window, I can shut it. When he enters my mind, I can cast him out. He becomes powerless when I take my power from You, Lord. You have given me the power to apprehend all of that and turn it around, just by living in Your truth of who I am.

You designed me to be a conqueror. You made me the head and not the tail. You designed me so that through Christ, I am made to win my race and am impossible to defeat. I was created to have a steadfast spirit, a spirit connected to You.

When I make use of Your name, Jesus, it is so powerful that it actually makes my enemies show themselves to me and brings peace to me when they slink from my life; sometimes, they do this in amazing displays of their hatred, and other times, they just simply disappear quickly and quietly.

I have learned that my enemies only have the power that I actually give them. I no longer have to live in prisons of comparison, jealously, envy, bitterness, or hatred. I do not need to tolerate joy-stealers, manipulators, vengeful thoughts, or revengeful people, within my own being or in the outside world.

But it is all through the power that You have given me. When I lean in to Your Spirit and am guided by Holy Spirit, I know that I am on the right path, regardless of what others may say. You did not give me the spirit of fear; that is from my enemy. You have given me Your Spirit and Your power, love, and a sound mind.

Jesus, You have set me free in every way and given me sight beyond what I can see. I can now identify more and more the spirits at war, and

I can cast out any evil spirits, those who come to kill, steal, and destroy what is being built up in You.

When I grasp Your vision, it gives me power and courage; You have restored power to the children of God and put us in our original place, having power over all living things. Praise You, Jesus, for the power you have given me.

~ ~ ~ ~

But indeed for this purpose I have raised you up, that I may show My power in you, and that My name may be declared in all the earth.
—Exodus 9:16 (NKJV)

He gives power to the weak, and to those who have no might He increases strength.
—Isaiah 40:29 (NKJV)

A final word: Be strong in the Lord and in his mighty power. Put on all of God's armor so that you will be able to stand firm against all strategies of the devil. For we are not fighting against flesh-and-blood enemies, but against evil rulers and authorities of the unseen world, against mighty powers in this dark world, and against evil spirits in the heavenly places.
—Ephesians 6:10–12 (NLT)

I can do all things through Christ who strengthens me.
—Philippians 4:13 (NKJV)

For God has not given us a spirit of fear and timidity, but of power, love, and self-discipline.
—2 Timothy 1:7 (NLT)

I Am ... Questioning

Regardless of our earthly age, we all come to You as little children. We all grow up in and with You, as we enter into and live in Your realm. Just as with human growth, we have spiritual growth, and I am really grateful, Lord, that You do not blast us all into oblivion when we ask questions, when we seek direction, and when we strive to learn. You gently and lovingly answer us all.

Each step with You opens up a new level of faith and of trust, and with me, it also opens up a new level of questioning and seeking within myself. That is not to say that I doubt You, because that is not the case. It's more a case of who You really are, as well as finding my bearings and where I am on this journey. You actually expect me to ask, to seek, and to question You. You created me with curiosity, and as I grow and question, You gift me with Your wisdom.

It is not a case of receiving the gift of my salvation from You and returning to my merry way of life. No, rather that is just the start of all You have prepared for me since before You created me.

As I walk with You, as You take my hand, we start this grand adventure of me asking You a lot of questions. Questions can show interest, involvement, desire, pursuit, and indeed doubt. There is a difference between asking questions like Your twelve disciples, who were eager to understand and know more, and the Pharisees, who wished to trap You with their questions.

While I have been guilty of testing You, over time, my doubt has diminished, my wisdom has increased, my faith and trust in You have grown, and my questions have become fewer, deeper, and more concise.

As I mature in Christ, You pour out more revelation, understanding, and wisdom onto me. You never expect me to know everything there is to know about You (nor about myself), but You do expect me to seek and question. And I am blessed to know that it is okay to question.

~ ~ ~ ~

But seek first the kingdom of God and His righteousness, and all these things shall be added to you.

—Matthew 6:33 (NKJV)

Ask, and it will be given to you; seek, and you will find; knock, and it will be opened to you. For everyone who asks receives, and he who seeks finds, and to him who knocks it will be opened.

—Matthew 7:7–8 (NKJV)

And whatever things you ask in prayer, believing, you will receive.

—Matthew 21:22 (NKJV)

One day some parents brought their little children to Jesus so he could touch and bless them. But when the disciples saw this, they scolded the parents for bothering him. Then Jesus called for the children and said to the disciples, "Let the children come to me. Don't stop them! For the Kingdom of God belongs to those who are like these children. I tell you the truth, anyone who doesn't receive the Kingdom of God like a child will never enter it."

—Luke 18:15–17 (NLT)

I Am ... Right Speaking

After years of hearing all the wrong voices being spoken to me and about me, it didn't take very long before I was thinking, believing, and indeed speaking all the wrong things about myself, Lord. I got to a point where I really no longer cared, even about myself. I rebelled, and rebelled hard, in my teens, but it was also in my teens that I had my first real encounter with You and Your love for me.

During this time, I accepted Your Son, Jesus Christ, into my heart. And just when I thought things might get better, I faced other voices, those from my friends who had accepted me as a messed-up teen. They were now the ones speaking the wrong voices over me because I had found God. I could not seem to win, Lord.

But as I have since learned, once You are in there, You do not leave. You were true to Your word when You said You would never leave me or forsake me. You were with me during the rest of my rebellion. You were there with me through my mistakes, trials, and errors, and indeed right through until today. You never did leave me.

I am so grateful that You remained faithful, Lord. That gave me a level of trust, of faith, to actually start getting to know You better and to get into what You have to say. When I started to understand more and actually started to speak Your word into myself and into my life, You sure did turn it all around for me. You are giving beauty for the ashes of my life, and You continue to do so. You take the dry bones of all I have done, the dead, the ugly, and make something beautiful, something I was created to be.

While I know that You are still working in me, and this journey is not over, it is amazing to me what You have already done with me. This is all just through listening to Your voice and speaking life, the life and promises You give me, to myself. I listen to how much You love me and accept me, and through right speaking, I am breaking all the bondage that is so deeply ingrained inside me. It was all through Your word and speaking it over my life.

Thank You, Lord, for giving me the hope, the encouragement, the power, and the strength that speaking Your word to myself gives me.

~ ~ ~ ~

The hand of the Lord was upon me, and He brought me out in the Spirit of the Lord and set me down in the middle of the valley; and it was full of bones. He caused me to pass all around them, and behold, there were very many human bones in the open valley; and lo, they were very dry. And He said to me, "Son of man, can these bones live?" And I answered, "O Lord God, You know." Again He said to me, "Prophesy to these bones and say to them, 'O dry bones, hear the word of the Lord.' Thus says the Lord God to these bones, 'Behold, I will make breath enter you so that you may come to life. I will put sinews on you, make flesh grow back on you, cover you with skin, and I will put breath in you so that you may come alive; and you will know that I am the Lord.'" So I prophesied as I was commanded; and as I prophesied, there was a thundering noise, and behold, a rattling; and the bones came together, bone to its bone. And I looked, and behold, there were sinews on the bones, and flesh grew and skin covered them; but there was no breath in them. Then He said to me, "Prophesy to the breath, son of man, and say to the breath, 'Thus says the Lord God, "Come from the four winds, O breath, and breathe on these slain, that they may live."'" So I prophesied as He commanded me, and the breath came into them, and they came to life and stood up on their feet, an exceedingly great army.

—Ezekiel 37:1–10 (AMP)

We call Abraham "father" not because he got God's attention by living like a saint, but because God made something out of Abraham when he was a nobody. Isn't that what we've always read in Scripture, God saying to Abraham, "I set you up as father of many peoples"? Abraham was first named "father" and then became a father because he dared to trust God to do what only God could do: raise the dead to life, with a word make something out of nothing. When everything was hopeless, Abraham believed anyway, deciding to live not on the basis of what he saw he couldn't do but on what God said he would do. And so he was made father of a multitude of peoples. God himself said to him, "You're going to have a big family, Abraham!"

—Romans 4:17–18 (MSG)

I Am ... Strong and Courageous

Let's face it, Lord: This world has become a pretty ugly place for so many. Yet in so many ways, it is still filled with so much beauty. Sometimes, I have to literally squint to see it, but it is there. Life happens still, and things try to knock me off course, but as I grow in and with You, these things that I face are not so much a temptation for me; they're more like a test that raises my godlike nature to the surface for me to actually see clearly.

I have to laugh sometimes, usually after I have overcome whatever it was, because these things are done for me to see more clearly. You already see it all and know it all, but You want me to see it too.

Adversity is going to hit me and, indeed, all people. I still have trials in my life, but I'm really learning to get Your perspective on them; You use them as effective tools to actually strengthen my faith and my relationship with You, and it takes me to a new level of trusting You. You use these things to strengthen me and make me courageous.

Your ways are indeed a mystery to me sometimes, but they are incredibly powerful. My strength will run out really quickly if I exclude You from my decisions. I ran this race called life for many years without You involved in it, and I was worn out by it all. I liken it to chasing my own tail or being on a hamster wheel; it just didn't end, and I seemed to get nowhere fast.

With You, including You in my day-to-day life, my choices and decisions, even just talking to You or humming a song in my head while I'm doing laundry or the dishes, things as simple as those mundane tasks, You strengthen me. You are in there with me in the knee-deep laundry, strengthening my spirit and singing back to my soul.

Knowing You're there in the little, silly stuff somehow gives me the strength and courage I need when I face the big things, the things I don't necessarily want to deal with, the things that come unexpectedly. You really do bless me with all this and make me so much stronger and more courageous than I could ever be on my own. With You and in You, I have the strength and courage to face all that life has to offer.

~ ~ ~ ~

Be strong and courageous, do not be afraid or tremble in dread before them, for it is the Lord your God who goes with you. He will not fail you or abandon you.

—Deuteronomy 31:6 (AMP)

Be of good courage, and He shall strengthen your heart, all you who hope in the Lord.

—Psalm 31:24 (NKJV)

The Lord God is my strength; He will make my feet like deer's feet, and He will make me walk on my high hills.

—Habakkuk 3:19 (NKJV)

The weapons we fight with are not the weapons of the world. On the contrary, they have divine power to demolish strongholds.

—2 Corinthians 10:4 (NIV)

Finally, be strong in the Lord and in his mighty power.

—Ephesians 6:10 (NIV)

You therefore, my son, be strong in the grace that is in Christ Jesus.

—2 Timothy 2:1 (NKJV)

Oh Lord, My God, You are my shepherd, and You are always with me. I know that You are here, whether I feel it or not, because Your word says so, and I trust Your word more than my feelings. You have marked me as Your creation, Your child, Your prize possession. You bought me with the price of the blood of Jesus, delivered me from darkness, and sealed me with Holy Spirit. When I go through valleys, I know that my stability comes from You. I need to go through things because if I choose to run from them, they just end up haunting me, and my fear of them grows. But with You, and my trust in You, I can actually make it through. You make me new and give me new life. You lead me on Your path to be right in Your eyes. You lift me up and restore my mind, body, soul, and spirit. You comfort me, and I become content in You. I am able to be at rest and have peace inside because of You and knowing that You are in control. My life is actually a whole lot easier when I surrender my control to You and choose Your will over my own. It is the power that is in Your word that corrects me, saves my soul, and heals me from the inside out. You have prepared so much for me, things to do and things to be; You anoint me by Your Spirit to do them. You bless me in so many ways. Your love, mercy, grace, and forgiveness are with me always. And I am so grateful that I get to live with You here, now and forever. Amen.

PART 5

I Am ... A Channel

I am so thankful that I do not have to let my experiences define who I am. I am not my past, and I am not my future, but I am a channel of everything I think, everything I feel, and everything I believe. All of that flows out of me into everything I do and everything I choose.

For too long, I allowed my past to dictate who I was; it trapped me in places I did not want to be, both internally and externally. If I thought little of myself, I found that I would end up in places where others thought little of me too. I was so used to being blamed that I blamed myself for everything. It was so wrong.

I used my past, and all that had happened, as a crutch to not succeed, virtually afraid of succeeding, in case I could not sustain it, because I was told I couldn't and wouldn't. What happened to me channeled out of me. I was a victim, not a victor.

But that isn't me, and that is not who I was created to be. You created me for more, and now I get to channel my life and my experiences as stepping stones, as a path to redemption, redemption in You, Lord.

With You and through You (and indeed, with You through me), my past is a channel to glory, to love, to forgiveness, to value, and to worth. I have found living water, and it flows from my heart out into my world. It is a channel of Your grace, Your peace, and Your love.

I am light, and I am salt. With each step, I am becoming a picture of You, right here and right now. I am what Your grace can do. I am constantly discovering new and interesting areas about my life, the stuff I once wanted to run from, that You are using to change me, change those around me, and change my little corner of this world.

There is nothing that You cannot use and that You cannot channel through. You take my brokenness and make it new. You take my ugliness and make it beautiful. You take my history and give it purpose. In all things, You create channels that point everything back to You.

~ ~ ~ ~

He cuts out channels in the rocks, and his eye sees every precious thing.

—Job 28:10 (NKJV)

Guard your heart above all else, for it determines the course of your life.

—Proverbs 4:23 (NLT)

Therefore I say to you, the kingdom of God will be taken from you and given to a nation bearing the fruits of it. And whoever falls on this stone will be broken; but on whomever it falls, it will grind him to powder.

—Matthew 21:43–44 (NKJV)

Whoever believes in me, as Scripture has said, rivers of living water will flow from within them.

—John 7:38 (NIV)

They will never again be hungry or thirsty; they will never be scorched by the heat of the sun. For the Lamb on the throne will be their Shepherd. He will lead them to springs of life-giving water. And God will wipe every tear from their eyes.

—Revelation 7:16–17 (NLT)

I Am ... Diligent

It took a long time to get into Your word, Lord. This whole journey actually started more with music. I saw a bumper sticker on one car, then another, then several, that simply named a local Christian radio station; I decided to tune in to see what it was all about. And I fell in love with the encouragement it gave. I had no idea modern faith-based music even existed. I would sing along with the songs, and the lyrics spoke to me. They lifted me up; they blessed me in some way and made me happier.

I then ventured out to actually buy a Bible. I thought that if this music was based on Your word, and there were indeed lyrics that I would pick up on and correlate to things I had heard as a child, yet they encouraged me, then maybe Your word wasn't actually as scary and horrific as I had come to believe all those years ago.

Lord, I have to say that no other book captivates or confuses more than Your word. For years, it confused me. I could not make sense of any of it. It was hard to read, it was hard to get into, it was just hard. It seemed like no matter how much I longed to be in it, I couldn't get into it. But You knew this, and You placed a couple of great people in my path to study Your word with, and they really helped. They brought some light and wisdom to Your word, and I started to see things. I am so grateful for those people, Lord.

Yet, I learned one very important lesson: It is a holy book, filled with Your Spirit, and it is only with Your Spirit that it will ever make any real sense and captivate me.

When I try on my own accord to make sense of it all, it makes little or no sense at all. Yet when I read it with You, You give me amazing clarity. The more clarity I have, the more time I want to spend in it and with You.

It also helps that without You in the mix, my enemies will never understand it. It is a powerful weapon, Lord, in the spiritual battle that we engage in. It is life-giving and vital and, let me also say, enjoyable.

While I am diligent to spend time with You, by means of Your word or just worshipping You, I love being with You each and every day.

~ ~ ~ ~

You show that you are a letter from Christ, the result of our ministry, written not with ink but with the Spirit of the living God, not on tablets of stone but on tablets of human hearts.

—2 Corinthians 3:3 (NIV)

I press toward the goal for the prize of the upward call of God in Christ Jesus.

—Philippians 3:14 (NKJV)

Practice and work hard on these things; be absorbed in them completely occupied in your ministry, so that your progress will be evident to all.

—1 Timothy 4:15 (AMP)

For if we are faithful to the end, trusting God just as firmly as when we first believed, we will share in all that belongs to Christ.

—Hebrews 3:14 (NLT)

Therefore, brethren, be even more diligent to make your call and election sure, for if you do these things you will never stumble; for so an entrance will be supplied to you abundantly into the everlasting kingdom of our Lord and Savior Jesus Christ.

—2 Peter 1:10–11 (NKJV)

I Am ... Filled with Peace

I have been fortunate enough, Lord, to lack for nothing in my life. Regardless of where I was, I somehow always had enough food (or money for food) and always had a roof over my head. Throughout my journey, I have come across those who didn't, yet they had something I lacked: peace.

Looking back, I cannot remember if it was just a peaceful acceptance they had or if it was real peace. I really didn't have either of those, and I longed for peace.

I thought if I had enough money, enough friends, enough of whatever, I would be able to accept where I was and that peace would just come. But that wasn't the case. Peace cannot be found in anything this world has to offer. We can accept where we are in this world and still not have peace; we just have acceptance, and the two are very different.

Even in my Christian walk, I have had acceptance but not peace. But through walking with You, I have discovered that my peace doesn't come from who or what I have; my peace comes from the One Who has me.

When I feed Your word into me, when I connect with You, when I pray and praise, I am actually getting out of Your way and allowing You to feed Your peace into me in bigger and greater ways. And it is indeed a true peace, a hard-to-describe peace, a peace that surpasses all human understanding. It can only be summed up as an experience, far different than acceptance or peace as we think we know it.

I can remember the very first time Your powerful peace came rushing across me and through me. It was like a tidal wave, filling every place in my body, mind, soul, and spirit, an overwhelming, indescribable event that to this day, I cling to.

Having Your peace and being in Your peace is now a compass for my life. If I don't feel it, I know that I am off-kilter somewhere, that I have somehow gotten out of Your will or indeed lost my connection with You; that maybe, just maybe I have inadvertently taken my own will back.

There are times when I really don't want to be where I am nor experience what I am, but I'm there for a reason: Your reason. And trusting in You brings peace to any situation I may find myself in.

Things are going to happen; trials will come, but trusting in You brings me peace. Peace is my strength. Peace is my power. Peace is actually my weapon, and it is a huge and mighty weapon. Trusting You brings me peace, Lord. I am incredibly grateful for the peace You give me.

~ ~ ~ ~

Peace I leave with you, My peace I give to you; not as the world gives do I give to you. Let not your heart be troubled, neither let it be afraid.
—John 14:27 (NKJV)

I have told you all this so that you may have peace in me. Here on earth you will have many trials and sorrows. But take heart, because I have overcome the world.
—John 16:33 (NLT)

The God of peace will soon crush Satan under your feet. The grace of our Lord Jesus be with you.
—Romans 16:20 (NIV)

Do not be anxious about anything, but in every situation, by prayer and petition, with thanksgiving, present your requests to God. And the peace of God, which transcends all understanding, will guard your hearts and your minds in Christ Jesus.
—Philippians 4:6–7 (NIV)

And let the peace of God rule in your hearts, to which also you were called in one body; and be thankful.
—Colossians 3:15 (NKJV)

I Am … Forgiving

Oh, goodness, yes! And I'm so grateful I am able to understand the true meaning of forgiveness through You, Lord. The unforgiving nature I had towards others, to myself, and also to You, Lord, kept me locked in this self-made prison; holding on to grudges, blame, and betrayal hardened my heart so much. It made me dead inside. And I had no idea I was even doing it.

I can flippantly say, "Forgive and forget," but I seemed to hold on to that little, tiny bit of whatever it was, and it grew within me. Whatever I have planted inside, grows—even if I'm not aware of it, until suddenly I am very aware of it, and I find myself trapped in a prison of hate.

I don't have to agree with what someone did or even with what I did to someone, but I need to forgive because it's forgiveness that destroys the prison I've built. And let's face it, I really don't agree with how I've been treated, which is why it caused hurt and pain—to me and indeed to them—but when I forgive and let it go, I grow. I can't control what has happened or what someone has done, but I can control me: my actions and my reactions.

So I now make the choice to shed the past, shed the yucky stuff, shed the hurt, and when I do, I am set free from it all, which allows room for the good stuff. When I forgive something, I can actually feel something in my heart grow. And it grows with love. Forgiving makes me strong, forgiving makes me bold, forgiving makes me loving.

I used to think that hanging on to that stuff made me bold and strong, but it doesn't; it was destroying me, totally wrecking me from the inside out. I have so many hurts from my past, and when I forgive them, as they cross my mind or as they happen in day-to-day life, I get this inner peace and hope and freedom, and a new wholeness comes across my entire being. It's a refreshing, clean feeling.

Forgiveness is such an amazing event; it happens inside of me yet empowers my outside. It sets me free to move forward with love and compassion. When I forgive, I can feel my spirit inside dance with joy. Forgiving others and myself changes my entire life.

I absolutely need to live in the manner that what Jesus has done for me is far, far greater than what anyone can do to me. And in that manner, I forgive, because I have been forgiven. And it is such a peaceful place to be.

Forgiveness is a two-way street; I can't give what I don't have, and because You freely gave it to me, I can give freely give it to others. Thank You, Jesus.

~ ~ ~ ~

And whenever you stand praying, if you have anything against anyone, forgive him, that your Father in heaven may also forgive you your trespasses.

—Mark 11:25 (NKJV)

And be kind to one another, tenderhearted, forgiving one another, even as God in Christ forgave you.

—Ephesians 4:32 (NKJV)

Make allowance for each other's faults, and forgive anyone who offends you. Remember, the Lord forgave you, so you must forgive others.

—Colossians 3:13 (NLT)

I Am ... Hopeful

In Proverbs, it says that hope deferred makes the heart sick. I always thought that meant that You were intentionally delaying everything I was hoping for because You wanted my heart to be sick; that's what religion did. But it isn't. What it means is that You don't want me to ever give up on hope. You want me to have desires in my heart and cling to hope because hope is what can take the not-so-good today and make tomorrow a better place. You also want my hope to find You and be placed in You.

Hope is indeed what got me through many days of chaos, abuse, and destruction. The hope that this was not the life I was meant to be living kept me going, kept me searching, kept me wanting peace in my world and indeed within myself. It was hope that kept me striving forward to become a better me. It was hope that kept me trying to see the good in any situation I faced. It was hope that finally left me on my knees in front of You.

I finally knew that I could not do any of this on my own, so I gave up my hope to You, in accepting You. And in return, You gave me a new hope, a hope of a real future, hope that my dreams would come true, hope that I would indeed find peace when I had none (none outside and certainly none inside).

I lived far too long in fear, ridicule, and shame, and You gave me real hope. When Christ was born, He was born to give me hope. When I read Your word, it gives me hope and encourages me. It's not that life is all of a sudden a bunch of roses with You; it's just that life with You means that You get to carry it all. I have a place to dump my stuff: my hopes, my dreams, my fears, my faith, my passions, my history, my future. I get to lay it all on You and, with hope and indeed faith, trust that You know what is best for me and that You will bring the best out of me.

Life with You gives me a confident hope now, not a desperate hope. This hope actually means my life is going to be all that it can be, and with my hope in You, I know that my hope is in a safe place, greater than I could imagine.

~ ~ ~ ~

For I know the thoughts that I think toward you, says the Lord, thoughts of peace and not of evil, to give you a future and a hope.

—Jeremiah 29:11 (NKJV)

Return to the stronghold, you prisoners of hope. Even today I declare that I will restore double to you.

—Zechariah 9:12 (NKJV)

Be joyful in hope, patient in affliction, faithful in prayer.

—Romans 12:12 (NIV)

Now may the God of hope fill you with all joy and peace in believing, that you may abound in hope by the power of the Holy Spirit.

—Romans 15:13 (NKJV)

This hope is a strong and trustworthy anchor for our souls. It leads us through the curtain into God's inner sanctuary.

—Hebrews 6:19 (NLT)

Let us hold unswervingly to the hope we profess, for he who promised is faithful.

—Hebrews 10:23 (NIV)

Now faith is the substance of things hoped for, the evidence of things not seen.

—Hebrews 11:1 (NKJV)

I Am ... Joyful

I gotta be honest, Lord. Sometimes, it's really hard to feel joyful when I see so much brokenness around me. There is so much hurt in this world, so much hate, so much destruction, and it hurts my heart. It hurts my heart even more when I see it in my own little corner of the world. I used to sit here and question You about it all. Like, where are You, God? Why are You letting all this stuff happen?

I'm starting to see that there may be a purpose to it all, like maybe we, Your children, are supposed to bring You to these situations wherever You guide us, or where situations we see just break our hearts. Isn't that part of the great commission and the grand plan? Our joy isn't supposed to come from this world; we are supposed to bring joy to this world. I think I'm getting it all now. My purpose here is to bring You to it, to shine Your light and Your joy, and in doing that, I get closer to You, and You actually help me to do all that.

My joy comes in the giving, just as Your joy did when You gave up Your life for me. I need to get my perspective right: My joy doesn't come from things or from others; it comes from You and literally giving You away to others. That makes me smile. That makes me happy. That brings me joy. And can I just say, Lord, that the closer I get to You, the happier I am.

The more I know You, the more I spend time with You, the more peace and joy I have. My life doesn't have to be perfect; I know I still face things I don't want to, and unexpected things happen, but I know You're in it all with me. I'm always with You, and even in storms, I can hang onto the joy that comes from just knowing You.

You have given me way more than I could have ever dreamed of, and I don't just mean in material things. I mean forgiveness, grace, mercy, and inner peace: things I can't buy. And the pure joy that comes from those things is just incredible.

You really do want us to be happy here on earth. Thank You for loving us so much that you gave everything for every single one of us, Lord. As our joy increases, help us bring joy to all that brokenness that remains. Everyone deserves to feel this way.

~ ~ ~ ~

"For I know the plans I have for you," says the Lord. "They are plans for good and not for disaster, to give you a future and a hope."
—Jeremiah 29:11 (NLT)

Instead of your former shame you will have a double portion; and instead of humiliation your people will shout for joy over their portion. Therefore in their land they will possess double what they had forfeited; everlasting joy will be theirs.
—Isaiah 61:7 (AMP)

But joyful are those who have the God of Israel as their helper, whose hope is in the Lord their God.
—Psalm 146:5 (NLT)

Until now you have not asked for anything in my name. Ask and you will receive, and your joy will be complete.
—John 16:24 (NIV)

But this I say: He who sows sparingly will also reap sparingly, and he who sows bountifully will also reap bountifully. So let each one give as he purposes in his heart, not grudgingly or of necessity; for God loves a cheerful giver.
—2 Corinthians 9:6–7 (NKJV)

I Am ... Loving

I never thought of myself as an unloving person, Lord; that is, until I realized just what the true meaning of love really was. I would care for people and have compassion and be kind and all that other stuff, but it never really amounted to any kind of real love. Not the kind You talk about and demonstrate, anyway.

I think when I entered into Your love, when I really started to experience what Your love really was, that's when I started to become a loving person and when I realized I didn't have a whole lot of love for even myself. I need to love me just as You love me, in order for me to be able to love anyone that You also love.

That was a hard road, learning to love myself, Lord. I had to leave abusive, toxic people and behaviors, theirs and mine, behind. I could not love myself trapped in situations that raped me of anything good I did have inside. I could not stay in hate and defeat and grow in love for myself. It just wasn't possible.

Yet You have shown me that I can still love those people. Love is an action, not a place. So praying for them, lifting them up to You and giving You the power over them, is indeed the most loving thing I could do. You are God, and I am not. Through growing in Your love for me, I have become a loving person.

I live generously and sincerely, and I forgive quickly and easily. I seek to understand rather than divide, and that has brought so many people closer in real love. I cling to what is good and pray over the rest, in myself and other people. I get out of the way and let You be God.

In our home, we are growing in Your love and wisdom, and each day, we try to live justly and honestly towards one another. What we do in our own hearts, and how we grow inside, through Your love, impacts our own person and filters out into the world outside. There is peace and unity within each of us when we truly love as You do.

It's like a circle: The more loving I am, the more joy I am blessed with, and the more joy I experience, the more loving I actually want to be. I don't think it's possible to love too much; there is no limit to Your love, so I continue to grow and be loving.

~ ~ ~ ~

Love must be sincere. Hate what is evil; cling to what is good.

—Romans 12:9 (NIV)

Love does no wrong to others, so love fulfills the requirements of God's law.

—Romans 13:10 (NLT)

Rather, he must enjoy having guests in his home, and he must love what is good. He must live wisely and be just. He must live a devout and disciplined life.

—Titus 1:8 (NLT)

They must not slander anyone and must avoid quarreling. Instead, they should be gentle and show true humility to everyone.

—Titus 3:2 (NLT)

Be hospitable to one another without grumbling.

—1 Peter 4:9 (NKJV)

This is real love—not that we loved God, but that he loved us and sent his Son as a sacrifice to take away our sins.

—1 John 4:10 (NLT)

I Am ... Surrendering

There is this incredible fear over the word "surrender." It's like if I surrender to whatever, I am giving up all my control. We are told to accept things. Acceptance will somehow bring harmony to our lives. We need to "accept who we are" or "accept that this is how it is" or "accept the past because we cannot change it."

Yet I have found that when I accept things like that, it actually keeps me trapped in that thought, that way, that mannerism, that personality. It does not set me free from anything; I just accept it as the way it is.

When I surrender, I actually set myself free from whatever it is. Surrender empowers me. I no longer need to worry about it or accept it. It relieves me of any expectations I have of myself or others have of me. I am free through surrendering.

Lord, I can spend my time spinning my wheels and trying in all my efforts to strive forward in this life, but I have found that surrender, and surrender to You, is what will free me from so many prisons—real and perceived. You offer me this grace and mercy. You offer to take all that I do not want and give me all that I need. I do not need to worry or seek control. I do not need to accept that this is just how it is, and I do not need to live under the illusion that surrender leaves me powerless.

You give me power through my surrender. It does not even matter if I am dealing with a thing, a situation, or other people. Surrender sets me free. Surrender actually takes any power away from whatever I was facing because I no longer face it. It takes the power away from those who wish to harm me or the thoughts that want to haunt me. Surrender lays it all down, Lord: my past, my present, my future, my blame, my shame, my hopes, and my dreams. Surrender gives it all to You.

In return, You give me grace, mercy, hope, balance, peace, harmony, a future, purpose, value, worth, and indeed forgiveness and joy, and all of that comes through surrender. Such an amazing and glorious place to be.

Thank You for all that comes through surrender and surrender to You.

With You, I am completely free with each and everything I surrender. I am so blessed by You.

~ ~ ~ ~

Happy are you, O Israel! Who is like you, a people saved by the Lord, the shield of your help and the sword of your majesty! Your enemies shall submit to you, and you shall tread down their high places.
—Deuteronomy 33:29 (NKJV)

The stuck-up fall flat on their faces, but down-to-earth people stand firm.
—Proverbs 11:2 (MSG)

Come to Me, all you who labor and are heavy laden, and I will give you rest. Take My yoke upon you and learn from Me, for I am gentle and lowly in heart, and you will find rest for your souls. For My yoke is easy and My burden is light.
—Matthew 11:28–30 (NKJV)

So humble yourselves before God. Resist the devil, and he will flee from you.
—James 4:7 (NLT)

Humble yourselves in the sight of the Lord, and He will lift you up.
—James 4:10 (NKJV)

I Am ... Thankful

Lord, I am thankful that nothing shocks You. Nothing I have ever done does, and nothing I will ever do is going to. You created and designed me; You were there before me, and You go before me. You are in my today and tomorrow. You already know. And when I rest in that knowledge, it's a good place to rest.

I no longer have to hide anything from You because You already know. You know all of my past, the things that I've done, the things that try to haunt me or distract me, and You give me a place to just leave them and walk away. That is amazing. But being grateful and thankful is so much more than that.

Gratitude comes from inside. It's being content, no matter what storms may be flying around outside of me. My true contentment and gratitude come from just being at peace, that peace that only You can give. Giving thanks to You even when I am struggling actually changes something inside of me; it's like I'm letting go of things, not concentrating on them, and just focusing on You instead. It changes the importance of bad circumstances or trials.

Over time, my gratitude towards You has also encompassed trust in You. It's not that I do nothing; it's just that in everything and with everything, I am grateful to You with the knowledge that You have whatever situation it is that I face. Whatever I achieve is because You gifted me in ways to achieve them. Whatever unexpected blessings I receive, they are blessings from You. You answer all of my prayers and all of my needs, always in Your perfect timing.

In times of trials, I can look back and see all that You have done for me throughout my entire life. I remember You and thank You for Your faithfulness then and go forward with the knowledge, experience, and trust that no matter what I face, You have it in Your very capable hands. I can simply think about my own salvation and what You gave to me and gave up for me.

The fundamental thing that this world cannot take from me is my freedom to choose and make my own decisions. I get to choose whether or not to be thankful, no matter where I am or what is happening, and I get to choose where I am going to place my thanks and gratitude. And I choose You. I choose to be grateful to the amazing, loving God Who made me and is always with me, no matter what.

No matter what I do, no matter where I go, whether I stay or leave, You are still here. And I am grateful.

~ ~ ~ ~

Enter into His gates with thanksgiving, and into His courts with praise. Be thankful to Him, and bless His name.

—Psalm 100:4 (NKJV)

Whatever you do no matter what it is in word or deed, do everything in the name of the Lord Jesus and in dependence on Him, giving thanks to God the Father through Him.

—Colossians 3:17 (AMP)

Rejoice always, pray without ceasing, in everything give thanks; for this is the will of God in Christ Jesus for you.

—1 Thessalonians 5:16–18 (NKJV)

A devout life does bring wealth, but it's the rich simplicity of being yourself before God. Since we entered the world penniless and will leave it penniless, if we have bread on the table and shoes on our feet, that's enough.

—1 Timothy 6:8 (MSG)

I Am ... Trusting

This is one topic I just do not like, Lord. It is hard. I have grown up with such mistrust that trusting anyone is extremely difficult for me. Trust is something that is built. It should be a growth thing ... with us all. It's a day-to-day, step-by-step, faith upon faith, prayer upon prayer, submission after submission type of thing.

Regardless of whether it is with another person or You, trust requires faith. And faith requires belief. And belief requires trust. I think all three go together in this nice, almost routine way, and all three require a relationship. The more I have faith in You, the more I believe in You, and the more I believe in You, the more I trust You. And You understand where I am, as well.

You actually provide so many opportunities for me to learn to trust You: small, little things which increase with time and intensity to greater and bigger things. You understand me and how I work, and You actually work with me. I'm grateful for that.

I am now in a place where trusting You is virtually second nature to me. You are like the eye in the storm, that calm place, where there is peace; trusting You while a storm is raging is safe. I admit that I can still waver—not often, but sometimes. It's through conversations with you, Lord, when I pray or just talk, when I exchange my thoughts and words and speak them to You, I build trust with You. Even though You know them already, it's like when I actually release them out of my mouth, a path of trust is being built.

I am learning that trusting You can and does break any fear I may feel because any worry I have is not going to add anything to my life; in fact, worry and fear just put faith in the wrong kingdom: the enemy's camp. Sometimes, I have to wait, and often I need to learn to wait better. With each experience, I understand more that the waiting period shows You exactly where my heart really is and whether I am going to doubt You or trust in You.

My willingness to trust You more is to choose Your will over my own. When I see Your perspective on things, when I grasp a glimpse of the bigger picture You are painting with everything that is going on, it is easier to trust; You are gracious to reveal things to me at the perfect time to actually reinforce my trust in You.

Thank You that You are so gracious and generous towards me; even in my weakness of trusting, You encourage me to grow in it. To me, that shows me someone worthy of my trust. Bless You, Lord.

~ ~ ~ ~

Trust in the Lord with all your heart, and lean not on your own understanding; in all your ways acknowledge Him, and He shall direct your paths.

—Proverbs 3:5–6 (NKJV)

Trust in the Lord and do good. Then you will live safely in the land and prosper. Take delight in the Lord, and he will give you your heart's desires. Commit everything you do to the Lord. Trust him, and he will help you.

—Psalm 37:3–5 (NLT)

I will say of the Lord, "He is my refuge and my fortress, my God, in whom I trust."

—Psalm 91:2 (NIV)

You will keep in perfect peace those whose minds are steadfast, because they trust in you. Trust in the Lord forever, for the Lord, the Lord himself, is the Rock eternal.

—Isaiah 26:3–4 (NIV)

Father God, You are the "I Am That I Am." You said it Yourself: the alpha and omega, the first and the last. You knew each one of us that was ever born before the foundation of the world, and You have a fabulous plan for each of our lives. Nothing that we have ever been through will be wasted. I am a living testimony to that, having been "missing in action" for about three decades before finally surrendering my whole being to You. You care so very deeply about every last detail of our lives, and You desire to mold and shape us to be more like Yourself. After all, we were made in Your image. And our prime directive is to get serious with You, with our lives, and You promised to help us be our best selves under Your workmanship, like the clay on the potter's wheel. We are to spread the news about how good You are, God. We thank You for being interested in us. Scripture says in Psalm 8:4 (NKJV), "What is man that You are mindful of him, and the son of man that You visit him?" We have a great big God, and He so wants an intimate relationship with each of us. To all who read this book, my heart's desire is that you are encouraged to seek His beautiful face; you won't recognize yourself after a time. We are each a work in progress, right up to the moment that He returns for us at long last. Blessings chase and overtake you all, everybody! In His great love, Amen.

—Margot Maines
Cowichan Valley, Vancouver
Island Canada

PART 6

I AM ... A DISCIPLE

When I think of the word "disciple," Lord, I can really get overwhelmed. I think that I need to have it all together, this life of perfection, almost without any flaws or mistakes. You gave me Your Son, Jesus, as my role model, and He was without blemish or flaws. I am so not that way, Lord.

Even today, after walking with You, studying Your word, and leaning in to Holy Spirit, I still make so many mistakes. I look at myself and do not see a disciple. But You do. You know, Lord, the strengths I have, and You use those strengths to grow me. You know my values, and while You can and will correct any that are off-kilter, You grow me in my values. You see someone who is devoted to learning and growing. You see someone who is committed and tries to be faithful to You and everyone else. That is what You see in me, Lord, and that is what You are using to make me a disciple.

In all that I do and in all that I say, I am a reflection of what I think and what I believe, and all that comes out, for the world to see. As I watch others, as I get inspiration from others, as I model others—whether they are good role models or not—I end up disciplining myself and those around me. My choices in the past may not have been great; in fact, some were downright awful, yet they have helped shape me into who I am today.

I made a decision to alter the course of my life many years ago. I made a decision then, which impacts my decisions today, which impacts those around me today. I am now able to use my experiences, from both sides of life, to either inspire others or drag them down.

My heart, Lord, is to inspire others and move them towards You. It is different than mentoring, Lord. It is a longing that whatever I do will have a lasting effect, leading way beyond me and my efforts; that I will be a launching pad, lifting others up who will then be a launching pad themselves, and with each launch, we get closer to Jesus and closer to You.

I realize now that I don't have to have everything figured out, and I don't have to live under the pressure of perfection; You take me where I am, with what I have, and You use me.

You teach me and make me Your disciple. With all that I am and all that I have been through, You turn it all for the good and the glory of Your kingdom, and I am so blessed to be involved in that. Thank You, Lord.

~ ~ ~ ~

And He said to them, "Follow Me as My disciples, accepting Me as your Master and Teacher and walking the same path of life that I walk, and I will make you fishers of men."

—Matthew 4:19 (AMP)

And Jesus came and spoke to them, saying, "All authority has been given to Me in heaven and on earth. Go therefore and make disciples of all the nations, baptizing them in the name of the Father and of the Son and of the Holy Spirit, teaching them to observe all things that I have commanded you; and lo, I am with you always, even to the end of the age." Amen.

—Matthew 28:18–20 (NKJV)

Jesus said to the people who believed in him, "You are truly my disciples if you remain faithful to my teachings. And you will know the truth, and the truth will set you free."

—John 8:31–32 (NLT)

A new command I give you: Love one another. As I have loved you, so you must love one another. By this everyone will know that you are my disciples, if you love one another.

—John 13:34–35 (NIV)

I Am ... Faithful

For most of my life, I seemed to be on a journey of escape: escape from rejection, from bullying, from fear, from my environment, and from myself. My journey of escape took me to anyone or anything that would accept me as I was. Of course, those were generally very unhealthy situations which actually propelled the downward spiral of trying to escape, making my escape just that much harder as I accumulated even more things I wanted to escape from.

Yet somewhere deep inside of me, I have always had faith. There was something that just kept me going, kept pushing me forward, and sometimes, it even kept me alive.

When I discovered Your faithfulness and Your love for me, the upward and forward journey to becoming faithful within myself started. It wasn't overnight, that's for sure. And it isn't over, either. But it's not hard being with You and in Your love. It's so easy; peaceful, even. Sometimes the road is narrow, but inside Your kingdom is vast.

The more I discover about You and how faithful You are to me, the more I want to be faithful not only to You, Lord, but also to all that You have given me. I don't want to be faithful because You are useful; I want to be faithful because You are beautiful! Faith is Your currency. It takes faith to see the unseen; often we are blind to who You are and what You actually do for us.

I believe You have been with me each and every step of my life. Things that should have killed me, haven't. Places I've put myself, places of great danger, I managed to get out of. When life should have taken me out, You kept me going. Great is Your faithfulness to me. The more I see that, the more my faithfulness towards You grows. When I step in to faith or indeed just remain faithful, You show up in amazing and unexpected ways, blessing me way more than I could have imagined.

You have never given up on me, and out of all the blessings You have given me, it is that—Your faith towards me, You never giving up on me—which keeps me faithful and keeps me pressing in! Thank You, Jesus.

~ ~ ~ ~

Oh, love the Lord, all you His saints! For the Lord preserves the faithful, and fully repays the proud person.
—Psalm 31:23 (NKJV)

The master was full of praise. "Well done, my good and faithful servant. You have been faithful in handling this small amount, so now I will give you many more responsibilities. Let's celebrate together!"
—Matthew 25:21 (NLT)

He who is faithful in what is least is faithful also in much; and he who is unjust in what is least is unjust also in much.
—Luke 16:10 (NKJV)

But what happens when we live God's way? He brings gifts into our lives, much the same way that fruit appears in an orchard—things like affection for others, exuberance about life, serenity. We develop a willingness to stick with things, a sense of compassion in the heart, and a conviction that a basic holiness permeates things and people. We find ourselves involved in loyal commitments, not needing to force our way in life, able to marshal and direct our energies wisely.
—Galatians 5:22–23 (MSG)

For whatever is born of God overcomes the world. And this is the victory that has overcome the world—our faith.
—1 John 5:4 (NKJV)

I Am ... Feasting and Fasting

I used to feast, and feast, and feast on all the world could give me. The good, the bad, and indeed the downright ugly. If I was hurt, I would hurt back. If I was betrayed, I would myself betray. If I was rejected, I found myself rejecting. Whatever happened to me, which as You know, Lord, was a lot of really messy, ugly stuff, I in turn would somehow feast on it inside myself and give it back to the world.

The same happened with the good things too, but interestingly enough, as I look back on my life, the good things seemed to take a lot longer to reproduce inside of me than the bad did. It took longer for me to show any love or anything virtuous.

It was almost like I was so used to bad things, that bad things were what came out of me so easily while I, within myself, craved the good things. Weird, huh? I really felt like I had no hope, yet something always kept me going, away from real death, the ending-my-life kind of death.

Today, even as I write this, I have tears in my eyes and a lump in my throat because I am now here and no longer there. My world has shifted; my world has changed. Today, I feast on You, and I fast on the world. Today, I stick close to You; I sink in to all You have to give me and all You have blessed me with: Your unrelenting love, Your unrelenting forgiveness, Your unrelenting grace and mercy. Those are what I feast on today.

I give up, let go of, and fast from the ugly, the bad, and the messy within me and indeed within others. You have helped me within my spirit, being connected to Your Spirit, to deal with the yucky things within me, of which there are many, to help me accept all that You have done, Your invitation to come, and that I'm worthy of You. You give me the ability to not ignore, but not concentrate on, those features in others.

Being an encourager and speaking life to someone means more to me today than ever before. You have made me what I always craved for from others in my life. And I'm so grateful.

I am grateful that my world has been turned around and that I crave to feast on all the goodness of who You are and indeed who I am in You, and that I no longer want, need, or feel I have to endure the world. I am indeed feasting on and fasting from, and that's an awesome place to be.

~ ~ ~ ~

A meal of bread and water in contented peace is better than a banquet spiced with quarrels.

—Proverbs 17:1 (MSG)

Is this not the fast that I have chosen: To loose the bonds of wickedness, to undo the heavy burdens, to let the oppressed go free, and that you break every yoke? Is it not to share your bread with the hungry, and that you bring to your house the poor who are cast out; when you see the naked, that you cover him, and not hide yourself from your own flesh? Then your light shall break forth like the morning, your healing shall spring forth speedily, and your righteousness shall go before you; the glory of the Lord shall be your rear guard. Then you shall call, and the Lord will answer; you shall cry, and He will say, "Here I am."

—Isaiah 58:6–9 (NKJV)

The servant returned and told his master what they had said. His master was furious and said, "Go quickly into the streets and alleys of the town and invite the poor, the crippled, the blind, and the lame." After the servant had done this, he reported, "There is still room for more." So his master said, "Go out into the country lanes and behind the hedges and urge anyone you find to come, so that the house will be full. For none of those I first invited will get even the smallest taste of my banquet."

—Luke 14:21–24 (NLT)

I Am ... Generous

The idea that I will reap what I sow has been so prevalent in my life, even from an early age. With all that went on around me, I was still a giver. In reality, I think I was a giver so that I could be a getter. I wanted love, so I gave love. There was a craving for something inside, a lack, so I gave what I wanted rather than what I had. I had no love, not even for myself, so how could I possibly give what I did not have? I encouraged because I wanted encouragement, but how could I truly know what that was if I had not experienced it myself?

Life with You has taught me so much about myself, Lord: where I was, where I want to be, and it has broken jagged pieces off so they no longer cut me and those around me. You have shown me that whatever is in my heart will flow from my heart; for way too long, that wasn't great stuff. I did not love You first; You loved me. You have loved me from the beginning of time, so through You, I have learned what true love actually is.

Through You, and through the death of Your Son for me, I have learned just what true giving and generosity are all about. Generosity is a heart condition. It is way more than giving, because it actually comes from the heart. Even those who were so opposed to the message of Your Son Jesus took care of widows and orphans, but they gave out of obligation, not from their hearts.

When I give with a generous heart, conviction says it should not matter who sees what I am doing, because I do things for others because I care deeply and passionately, and that is all that matters. I no longer give to receive, and I no longer give to be seen. When I am generous, I am free, because Jesus said I am more blessed giving than receiving. I give because it is a desire, a passion, a plan, and indeed my purpose. You are the only One Who truly sees my heart and my motives; You see everything, Lord.

When my heart is in the right place, You will provide. You will bless. You will raise me up according to Your will, Your purpose, and Your glory.

And You will do it all when my heart is indeed in the right place and its compass points in the right direction: away from me. Bless You, Lord.

~ ~ ~ ~

Guard your heart above all else, for it determines the course of your life.
—Proverbs 4:23 (NLT)

For where your treasure is, there your heart will be also.
—Matthew 6:21 (NKJV)

Give, and it will be given to you. They will pour into your lap a good measure—pressed down, shaken together, and running over with no space left for more. For with the standard of measurement you use when you do good to others, it will be measured to you in return.
—Luke 6:38 (AMP)

Let each one give thoughtfully and with purpose just as he has decided in his heart, not grudgingly or under compulsion, for God loves a cheerful giver and delights in the one whose heart is in his gift.
—2 Corinthians 9:7 (AMP)

Do not be deceived: God cannot be mocked. A man reaps what he sows. Whoever sows to please their flesh, from the flesh will reap destruction; whoever sows to please the Spirit, from the Spirit will reap eternal life. Let us not become weary in doing good, for at the proper time we will reap a harvest if we do not give up.
—Galatians 6:7–9 (NIV)

I Am ... Generational

Thinking of myself as generational is a strange concept, Lord. I used to be such an incredibly selfish person: all about me, my needs, and my wants. Living paycheck to paycheck, at times without paychecks, scrambling for this or that; life was all about the here and now.

In fact, we are told we are supposed to live "in the now". But where on earth does now even come in to generations—future generations? Yet it does, and I see that so much more clearly now.

Everything I do now affects my tomorrow. In fact, it affects so many tomorrows for people I don't even know yet. I am trying to raise my children to be the best they can be at whatever they choose to be, to go with their strengths and their passions, and indeed I'm learning to do the same with myself. And while all of that is going to affect any grandchildren I may be blessed with, it comes closer to home than even that. It is going to affect all the people they come across in their lives, their friends at school right now, future relationships and friendships, their peers at work or college. Whatever I do now affects their tomorrows, their friends' tomorrows, and their friends' friends' tomorrows.

I can look back on my past and my behaviors and wonder just how much they changed the worlds of those whose paths I crossed way back then. How much did my rebellion affect my parents or my family? How much did it affect the friends of those people? Everything I do now, everything I did then, and indeed everything I do from this point onwards, affects (or affected) someone.

This is not only something You always knew, Lord, but it is also a scientifically proven fact, known as the Butterfly Effect. And You actually knew this at the beginning of time, Lord. You knew when You created each and every living thing with the ability to reproduce. Whatever I do, whatever I think, whatever I believe, will reproduce and manifest itself outside of me.

Oh Lord, I have been so blind to this in so many ways. I understood how all of this affects me, but how blind have I been to how it affects others? I am a generational being, whether I like it or not.

My choices and my decisions are going to live on long after I leave this earth. Each and every thing I do affects so many, who I may never even know. It is no wonder to me now why You prune us to get rid of the rotten and dead things. You do it because You love each and every one of us, here and now and indeed those to come.

Your desire is for everyone to flourish and no one to die. Thank You, Lord, for the revelation of generations and for making me a generational being. Please help me grow in this area.

~ ~ ~ ~

Then God said, "Let the land sprout with vegetation—every sort of seed-bearing plant, and trees that grow seed-bearing fruit. These seeds will then produce the kinds of plants and trees from which they came." And that is what happened.

—Genesis 1:11 (NLT)

Your wife shall be like a fruitful vine in the very heart of your house, your children like olive plants all around your table.

—Psalm 128:3 (NKJV)

I am the true vine, and My Father is the vinedresser. Every branch in Me that does not bear fruit He takes away; and every branch that bears fruit He prunes, that it may bear more fruit. You are already clean because of the word which I have spoken to you.

—John 15:1–3 (NKJV)

Yes, I am the vine; you are the branches. Those who remain in me, and I in them, will produce much fruit. For apart from me you can do nothing. Anyone who does not remain in me is thrown away like a useless branch and withers. Such branches are gathered into a pile to be burned.

—John 15:5–6 (NLT)

I Am ... Gracious

It took me a while to even start understanding grace, let alone acting with it, and I am sorry, Lord. I can get so trapped in comparing myself and my walk to that of other people that I actually put blinders on to the grace You have shown to me. I see their perceived outward success and wonder why I feel trapped; why am I not seeing success in the same way, or I have that same gift; why aren't You using me, God? It's silly. In fact, it's downright dumb.

You have shown such grace to me in so many ways. You gave up Your Son for all my sins as well as eternal life with You, not forgetting Holy Spirit, who is with me at all times. You show it to me each and every day in ways I often cannot see until after the fact.

Grace and graciousness to others is just appreciating that they too have a walk and a journey; they have their lane in the road, and I have mine.

Lord, sometimes I would feel like Jonah, hating those "over there" because I didn't like what they're doing or I didn't agree with how they live. And it is hard, really hard, to show grace to those who have really hurt us. It sometimes takes everything in us to do it. But it's necessary ... hard but necessary.

I so need to live by Your example of grace because left to myself and my own devices, I would fail miserably. You love them just like You love me. You want to show Your grace to us all, and that means I need to be gracious too. I am here to show Your grace, not to feel important or better than or holier than thou, but to be like Jesus, who humbled Himself before me, suffered for me, so that I could live in Your kingdom.

So I walked, and continue to walk, through many lessons about graciousness. And with each step I take, through each fear I face, through each prideful wall I tear down, I became more and more gracious.

I am so grateful for the learning process. It has changed me and my family. It has changed how just this small nucleolus of people interact with each other. Being gracious is such a blessing, and as we continue to grow in Your grace, we are able to be so much more gracious to others. It is liberating, and I thank You, Jesus, for being such an incredible example of graciousness.

~ ~ ~ ~

God said, "What's this? How is it that you can change your feelings from pleasure to anger overnight about a mere shade tree that you did nothing to get? You neither planted nor watered it. It grew up one night and died the next night. So, why can't I likewise change what I feel about Nineveh from anger to pleasure, this big city of more than 120,000 childlike people who don't yet know right from wrong, to say nothing of all the innocent animals?"

—Jonah 4:10–11 (MSG)

For by the grace of God given to me I say to every one of you not to think more highly of himself and of his importance and ability than he ought to think; but to think so as to have sound judgment, as God has apportioned to each a degree of faith and a purpose designed for service.

—Romans 12:3 (AMP)

But we do see Jesus, who was made lower than the angels for a little while, now crowned with glory and honor because he suffered death, so that by the grace of God he might taste death for everyone.

—Hebrews 2:9 (NIV)

Therefore, since we are receiving a kingdom which cannot be shaken, let us have grace, by which we may serve God acceptably with reverence and godly fear.

—Hebrews 12:28 (NKJV)

I Am ... Praying and Praising

I think most of us pray. I think we always have. But somehow our prayers are more like wishes we hope will come true rather than believing they actually will. As a child, I would pray for this or that at Christmas; as a teen, it was probably about some boy I had a crush on, and as I got older and was without You in my life, it was just that I wouldn't mess this up.

Indeed, I think we have always praised, but again, without real belief or heart, more a glib or dismissive "Thank God" as we find out a disaster in our lives has been averted; I know I sure did.

As a Christian, with You in my life, my prayer life didn't change much, except I started to pray about others as well as myself. But still, they were more wishes than things I really believed You could deliver. I still don't think I understand it all, but I sure understand more than I did, and prayer today is one of the best weapons I have.

When I pray with belief attached to it, when I actually believe that You can and will deliver, I stop the enemy dead in his track and take his power away.

Prayer is communication as well as declaration. Prayer allows me to communicate in a very real and honest way all that I know to be in my heart, and even though You know my heart already, I think You want me to speak it out, because in speaking it out, I get to hear it too. Prayer and praise for You somehow unblocks things inside of me which hinder all that You want to bring to me and through me. Prayer is a form of letting go of all that I am and giving it all to You: the good, the bad, and the ugly. You use it all. You refresh all the parts of me that need new life and a new breath.

When I praise, it is all about the sacred relationship I have with You, Lord, because it is all about You. I come to You, I seek You, and I yearn to find You, and it is done with my heart. Not my mind, my will, or my emotions, but my heart.

You care more about my heart condition than any other part of my being. What I carry in my heart is who I am. Sometimes, that's not very good, but through this process, You get to change it in a way that I do not necessarily understand, but I don't need to. Praying to you and praising You for all You have done (and all You will ever do) is a communication that purges the ugliness from me and makes me truly alive and indeed grateful for where I am, no matter what.

~ ~ ~ ~

Make a joyful shout to the Lord, all you lands! Serve the Lord with gladness; come before His presence with singing. Know that the Lord, He is God; it is He who has made us, and not we ourselves; we are His people and the sheep of His pasture. Enter into His gates with thanksgiving, and into His courts with praise. Be thankful to Him, and bless His name.

—Psalm 100:1–4 (NKJV)

Then you will call on me and come and pray to me, and I will listen to you. You will seek me and find me when you seek me with all your heart.

—Jeremiah 29:12–13 (NIV)

Do not be anxious about anything, but in every situation, by prayer and petition, with thanksgiving, present your requests to God. And the peace of God, which transcends all understanding, will guard your hearts and your minds in Christ Jesus. Finally, brothers and sisters, whatever is true, whatever is noble, whatever is right, whatever is pure, whatever is lovely, whatever is admirable—if anything is excellent or praiseworthy—think about such things.

—Philippians 4:6–8 (NIV)

I Am ... Resting in Christ

Just like in my human life, I go through growth stages in my spiritual life. We come to You as little children, babies, and we learn to sit, stand, walk, run, and indeed rest.

I spent the majority of my life running. Running from all that I had endured and indeed running even from myself. Someone once told me that no matter where I ran to, I took myself with me, and I found that very profound. It really doesn't matter what I was running from; I still had all the stuff I carried inside with me. Resentments, anger, mistrust, lack of love, fear: It was all there, harbored in my heart and devouring my soul each and every day. It was what I believed kept me safe from the world. The world, I had discovered, was not always a nice, cozy, loving place, and so I tried to run from it. Yet I took all of that with me when I did. My world outside had become my world inside.

When I started to walk with You, I started to slowly shed all that stuff. It didn't happen instantly, and indeed I can remember more than one occasion when You were asking me to let go, and I fought You to hang on; that was a painful experience. If I had just let go, it would have been gone. But in my world, and indeed in my heart, at that time, holding on to stuff is what I *thought* kept me safe.

You never gave up, though. You knew that I could not have genuine peace and freedom, carrying all that I was carrying, and eventually showed me that I had found a place not of this world, where I could place it all: at Your feet. I started to let go. I started to surrender. I started to have faith and trust in You. As I let go, You filled those places with peace. I no longer had all this junk around my heart and in my mind, haunting me daily.

You brought me to a place of rest, real rest, a rest where no matter what is going on outside, I can be with You and at rest in You on my inside: in my mind and in my heart. When I truly rest in Christ, I am actually allowing You to direct my heart into more of Your love through Christ.

So much of my life was filled with worry, anxiety, and fear, and all of that just steals life away from me. It never solves anything, and it just grows into more worry, anxiety, and fear. With You, though, when I am resting in You, I am trusting You with all my circumstances and trials.

I no longer need to run away; I just come and rest at Your feet, giving all my worries and burdens to You. What an awesome place to be. Thank You, Lord.

~ ~ ~ ~

Rest in the Lord, and wait patiently for Him; do not fret because of him who prospers in his way, because of the man who brings wicked schemes to pass.

—Psalm 37:7 (NKJV)

Then Jesus said, "Come to me, all of you who are weary and carry heavy burdens, and I will give you rest. Take my yoke upon you. Let me teach you, because I am humble and gentle at heart, and you will find rest for your souls. For my yoke is easy to bear, and the burden I give you is light."

—Matthew 11:28–30 (NLT)

Therefore, while the promise of entering His rest still remains and is freely offered today, let us fear, in case any one of you may seem to come short of reaching it or think he has come too late.

—Hebrews 4:1 (AMP)

I Am ... Serving with Purpose

No matter what goes on inside of me, it eventually ends up coming out for both me and the world to see. It always does. I used to think that no one would know. But here's the thing I discovered: I knew. And it ate away at me inside. I knew that what I was doing and who I was becoming was not the me I wanted to be. In fact, it was so far away from the me I wanted to be, it wasn't funny.

Slowly, over time, all the stuff I harbored inside—my thoughts, my feelings, my emotions—spilled out. They spilled out in anger, mistrust, and unforgiveness, and it wasn't pretty. It was directed towards myself and others.

It took time for all that to change, and the only way it has changed is life with You. Some things are instantaneous: salvation and forgiveness, for instance. But others take time: unlearning everything I have become and becoming everything I was meant to be. It's a journey, and I am still on it, but I'm on it with You.

My life is more than just mimicking good and godly outward behaviors; my life is what is happening inside of me, being transformed by Your spirit, so that You show on the outside. You have a design for every life, and indeed there is a purpose for everything under heaven.

So many people think that it is all about religion or religious ceremony, but it's not. It is completely and totally relational. And all relationships involve levels of intimacy and vulnerability, no matter who they are with: with You or with others. Each step of being vulnerable takes me to a deeper level with You (and also with me). Each step involves letting go and making room for You to breathe in me. And each step has led me to today and to a life committed to speaking life, not death, to myself and others.

I still falter, and I'm not perfect, but I'm progressing, and I'm determined that the more I am committed to serving with loving, life-giving words, the more hurt will vanish from my world.

No one is going to see You if I hide myself away. No one is going to see You if I hide behind the religiosity You came to get rid of, but everyone will see You through my relationship with You. You created me to serve, and You created me for a purpose. I am no longer living with sight but no vision. I am living with the vision You created before You wrapped me around it.

My purpose is to shine in this world, to actually be light in the darkness and let the world see You. And with everything I do, and indeed with the intimate desires in my heart, You somehow, and in Your time, make them succeed forward, outward, and inward.

~ ~ ~ ~

But if serving the Lord seems undesirable to you, then choose for yourselves this day whom you will serve, whether the gods your ancestors served beyond the Euphrates, or the gods of the Amorites, in whose land you are living. But as for me and my household, we will serve the Lord.

—Joshua 24:15 (NIV)

For I know the thoughts that I think toward you, says the Lord, thoughts of peace and not of evil, to give you a future and a hope.

—Jeremiah 29:11 (NKJV)

May he grant your heart's desires and make all your plans succeed.

—Psalm 20:4 (NLT)

For we are His workmanship, created in Christ Jesus for good works, which God prepared beforehand that we should walk in them.

—Ephesians 2:10 (NKJV)

And those he predestined, he also called; those he called, he also justified; those he justified, he also glorified.

—Romans 8:30 (NIV)

I AM ... WATCHFUL

I don't know where to begin on being watchful, Lord, because I never used to be. It was just something I don't feel I did until I got much older. And then, it was a cynical watchful, not a faithful watchful. It was a suspicious and fearful watchful, self-protective, not generous or kind, and it certainly wasn't built on any kind of love or faith. Having been betrayed so many times, and of course without forgiveness in my heart, I found myself living in a different kind of prison I built for myself. I think now, as I look back, that had I had any kind of real love or compassion for both them and myself, my "watchful" would have looked a whole lot different.

Yes, we have an enemy who seems very alive and well in our world, who wants to take us out and stop any progress we are trying to make in our health, our wealth, and indeed our inward prosperity. And being aware of that makes us watchful, but it should not make us suspicious of everyone we meet, leaving us wondering what their ulterior motive is or why they could possibly be interested in talking to us.

The amazing thing is that I have been blessed with Holy Spirit, and He is my watchtower now. And You send beacons off within me when I'm not as alert as I should be or indeed before I even get to a danger stage. The closer I get to You, the more I'm in You and You're in me, the more aware I actually am of things. It seems to come naturally now, so that I can spot danger, deceit, and dishonesty a mile off and have the ability to truly stand where I am, firmly in Your presence, when enemy spirits come to attack, both inwardly and outwardly.

Occasional attacks from enemy spirits flow like water from a duck's back, and consistent attacks are cut off at the ankles so they no longer have any effect. Being rooted in You and continuously growing in You has raised me up and given me the ability to be watchful in a very solid, trusting, and indeed loving way. Attacks are now prayed over instead of worried over, and I am able to lift people up to You and get out of Your way.

People and spirits can still hurt, especially if we perceived that they should have been more loyal or genuine, Christ-follower or not, but I'm thankful, Jesus, that I am now watchful in a new and better way.

~ ~ ~ ~

Stay alert. This is hazardous work I'm assigning you. You're going to be like sheep running through a wolf pack, so don't call attention to yourselves. Be as cunning as a snake, inoffensive as a dove.

—Matthew 10:16 (MSG)

So then, since we have a great High Priest who has entered heaven, Jesus the Son of God, let us hold firmly to what we believe.

—Hebrews 4:14 (NLT)

Look after each other so that none of you fails to receive the grace of God. Watch out that no poisonous root of bitterness grows up to trouble you, corrupting many.

—Hebrews 12:15 (NLT)

So keep at your work, this faith and love rooted in Christ, exactly as I set it out for you. It's as sound as the day you first heard it from me. Guard this precious thing placed in your custody by the Holy Spirit who works in us.

—2 Timothy 1:13–14 (MSG)

Stay alert! Watch out for your great enemy, the devil. He prowls around like a roaring lion, looking for someone to devour.

—1 Peter 5:8 (NLT)

I Am ... Wise

There's a difference between smart and wise, and between experience and wisdom, and most certainly between knowledge and wisdom. I get now why You dedicated more than a whole book in Your Word to wisdom. It makes sense now.

I was so often "wise in my own eyes," especially as a rebellious teenager. The things I thought I was doing right, well, I really wasn't. It's not like everything I did was wrong, but even in my rightness, I'm not sure I was making the best choices for my life.

I sure do wish I had all Your wisdom back then. I could have avoided so many potholes in my road. With You, Lord, nothing is too bad for You, nothing is too deep for You, nothing is too messy for You. No matter where I find myself or indeed where anyone finds themselves, You are so willing and actually want to roll up Your sleeves and pick us up out of the swamp and just pour Your love and wisdom on us.

I don't make me right; You do. When I stick close to You, especially in and through Your word, You seep into my spirit and soul. And before I even realize it, my life has changed. At first in small ways, but then in bigger and greater ways. And it's not like the journey ever ends. It's not like I will ever know everything there is to know. But the closer I stay to You, the better a person I become.

I am in a place now where I do not want to go anywhere in life without Your instruction and guidance. I use the peace I feel from You as a major guiding factor, and that peace comes only from Holy Spirit, who connects the dots all the way back to You. Recklessness is a faraway place from me now, and I am wise enough to know that my rock, my foundation, is indeed You.

~ ~ ~ ~

Those who are wise shall shine like the brightness of the firmament, and those who turn many to righteousness like the stars forever and ever.

—Daniel 12:3 (NKJV)

Many shall be purified, made white, and refined, but the wicked shall do wickedly; and none of the wicked shall understand, but the wise shall understand.

—Daniel 12:10 (NKJV)

Do not be wise in your own eyes; fear the Lord and shun evil.

—Proverbs 3:7 (NIV)

Listen to my instruction and be wise. Don't ignore it.

—Proverbs 8:33 (NLT)

The fruit of the righteous is a tree of life, and the one who is wise saves lives.

—Proverbs 11:30 (NIV)

He who heeds the word wisely will find good, and whoever trusts in the Lord, happy is he.

—Proverbs 16:20 (NKJV)

The wise are mightier than the strong, and those with knowledge grow stronger and stronger.

—Proverbs 24:5 (NLT)

Anyone who listens to my teaching and follows it is wise, like a person who builds a house on solid rock.

—Matthew 7:24 (NLT)

So be careful how you live. Don't live like fools, but like those who are wise.

—Ephesians 5:15 (NLT)

AFTERWORD

As I travel this journey with Jesus, I come across many other Jesus-followers, and my discovery has been that each and every one of us is on our own very personal path. It is unlikely that you are where I am, because while we can have similar experiences, we can still come from different places. Our journeys are unique. God designed us that way.

We are growing, spiritual beings, and we were designed to grow in and through our victory in Christ. We are the head, not the tail; we are victors, not victims. Our past and our today are merely stepping stones towards our tomorrow and our future. Your journey is not over, and neither is mine. I am still growing and changing and learning, and that will never end. There is beauty in that.

I still face trials in my life; that is unlikely to change, but my perspective of them has. I do not need to worry, and I do not need to fear; I just need to lean in more to the One Who saved me. A test will lead me towards God; a temptation will lead me away. I know which path I want to choose, because I know which path is loving, safe, and secure.

I hope that no matter where you are and no matter what you might be facing, you will have found a jewel or a nugget in this book that you can relate to or cling to. I pray that somehow, something has reached out to you to give you hope. Hold on to that, guard it, and let no one steal it from you. It does not matter if it was one word, one relatable experience, or one scripture noted. Hold on to it deep in your heart, and I promise you that with that one small seed, God will grow it. You will see over time that God will use that to add more, increase it, and love you with it. It's just what He does. He is faithful, and He loves you, right where you are.

Adriene

SPEAK LIFE OVER YOURSELF AND BLESS YOURSELF

This is a small collection of some of the verses I have chosen to speak over my life, in my own words. The scripture references beside each one points to the original scriptures, which were taken from the New King James Version of the Bible.

God made me in His image and likeness; He gave me dominion over everything, including my own choices. He blesses me with everything. (Genesis 1:26–28)

I trust in God with all my heart, and even when things don't make sense, I know He is directing my path. (Proverbs 3:5–6)

God is my refuge and my strength. He is my very present help in times of trouble. Therefore, I will not fear. (Psalm 46:1)

I can call on God at any time: morning, noon, or night. I can cry and pray out loud, and He hears me. He redeems my soul and gives me peace from whatever battle I'm facing. (Psalm 55:16–18)

I am planted in the house of the Lord, and I will flourish in His courts forever. (Psalm 92:13)

I am praising God because He made me wonderful and marvelous, and that my soul knows very well. (Psalm 139:14)

God's thoughts for me are good and glorious. If I could count them, they would be greater than all the grains of sand on a beach. (Psalm 139:17)

God has a purpose for everything, and His hand is stretched out towards me; I will not turn back. (Isaiah 14:27)

When I rest in the Lord, He renews my strength. He gives me energy to soar like the eagles, breath to run and not pass out, strength to walk and not faint. He is my source and my strength. (Isaiah 40:31)

God knew me before I was formed in my mother's womb. Before I was born, He sanctified me and gave me a purpose. (Jeramiah 1:5)

God's thoughts for me are good. They give me hope and a future. (Jeremiah 29:11)

I am seeking God first and His kingdom and His righteousness, and everything I need is being added to me. (Matthew 6:33)

I am more valuable to God than the birds. He knows every hair that is and was ever on my head. (Matthew 10:30–31)

God gives me somewhere to come to when the world gets me down. His burden is light, and He takes all my worries. (Matthew 11:28)

Through the acceptance of Jesus, I became a child of God. (John 1:12)

Jesus came as a light into this world so that I would not need to live in bondage or darkness. (John 12:46)

Jesus is the tree, and I am a branch. When I stay in the tree, growing from the tree, I will bear good fruit and all good things. (John 15:5)

This world may try to shake me and send trials my way, but I have peace in those trials and courage because I am in Christ, and He overcame them all. (John 16:33)

The love of God has been poured over me into my heart by Holy Spirit, who was given to me freely. His hope does not disappoint. (Romans 5:5)

The Spirit of God, who raised Jesus from the dead, lives within me. He who raised Christ gives me new life through His Spirit. (Romans 8:11)

I am more than a conqueror with Christ. There is nothing I cannot overcome, and nothing can separate me from God's love for me. (Romans 8:37–39)

I am no longer conformed to the patterns of this world. I am being transformed by the renewing of my mind. (Romans 12:2)

Through Christ, I have been anointed, sealed, and given Holy Spirit in my heart as a guarantee that God is always with me. (2 Corinthians 1:21)

I walk by faith and not by sight. (2 Corinthians 5:7)

In Christ, I have redemption through His blood and the forgiveness of all my sins, according to the riches of His grace, which He makes abound towards me. (Ephesians 1:7–8)

I am His workmanship, created in Christ Jesus, for good works, which God Himself prepared for me. (Ephesians 2:10)

I have been set apart by God. I worship in Spirit and rejoice in Christ. He is my confidence. (Philippians 3:3)

The peace of God that I don't yet fully understand is guarding my heart and my mind in Christ Jesus. (Philippians 4:7)

Christ has delivered me from the power of darkness and placed me in His kingdom, and through His blood, I have redemption and forgiveness for all I have ever done. (Colossians 1:13–14)

I am devoting myself to prayer, being watchful, and being thankful. (Colossians 4:2)

I am fixing my eyes on Jesus. He is the One Who makes my faith perfect. (Hebrews 12:2)

Jesus Himself took all of my sin onto His own body when He was nailed to the cross so that having died to sin, I could truly live and live righteously, knowing that God is not mad at me and that God loves me. It is by the wounds that Jesus took that I am healed. (1 Peter 2:24)

www.IdentityCrisisUndone.org

Follow us on Facebook:
www.facebook.com/identitycrisisundone
or
www.facebook.com/speakpromises

May God richly bless you
so that you prosper
as your soul prospers!